Wisconsin's Recreational Bicycle Trails

An
American Bike Trails
Publication

Wisconsin's Recreational Bicycle Trails

Published by American Bike Trails
610 Hillside Avenue
Antioch, IL 60048

Created by   Ray Hoven
Designed by   Mary C. Rumpsa

Table of Contents

Table of Contents (continued)

How To Use This Book

This book provides a comprehensive, easy to use quick reference to the many recreational trails throughout the state of wisconsin. It contains over 60 detailed trail maps, plus southern, central, and northern wisconsin sectional map overviews. Each trail map includes such helpful features as location and accesses, trail facilities, and nearby communities. The trails in the book are organized in alphabetical order. The back of the book includes a cross-reference listing of trails by county and town, and a listing and description of alternative mountain bike trail opportunities.

Terms Used

Bicycle Trail	An off-road path designated as open to bicycling.
Bikeway	A shoulder, street or sidewalk recommended as a bicycle route.
Alternate Bike Trail	An off-road trail other than the one featured on a map illustration.
Directions	Describes by way of directions and distances, how to get to the trail areas from roads and nearby communities.
DNR	Department of Natural Resources
Forest	Typically encompasses a dense growth of trees and underbrush covering a large tract.
Length	Expressed in miles. Round trip mileage is normally indicated for loops.
Map	Illustrative representation of a geographic area, such as a state, section, forest, park or trail complex.
Park	A tract of land generally including woodlands and open areas.

Types of Biking

Mountain	Fat-tired bikes are recommended. Ride may be generally flat but then with a soft, rocky or wet surface.
Leisure	Off-road gentle ride. Surface is generally paved or screened.
Tour	Riding on roads with motorized traffic or on road shoulders.

Riding Tips

- Pushing in gears that are too high can push knees beyond their limits. Avoid extremes by pedaling faster rather than shifting into a higher gear.

- Keeping your elbows bent, changing your hand position frequently and wearing bicycle gloves all help to reduce the numbness or pain in the palm of the hand from long-distance riding.

- Keep you pedal rpms up on an uphill so you have reserve power if you lose speed.

- Stay in a high-gear on a level surface, placing pressure on the pedals and resting on the handle bars and saddle.

- Lower your center of gravity on a long or steep downhill run by using the quick release seat post binder and dropping the saddle height down.

- Brake intermittently on a rough surface.

- Wear proper equipment. Wear a helmet that is approved by the Snell Memorial Foundation or the American National Standards Institute. Look for one of their stickers inside the helmet.

- Use a lower tire inflation pressure for riding on unpaved surfaces. The lower pressure will provide better tire traction and a more comfortable ride.

- Apply your brakes gradually to maintain control on loose gravel or soil.

- Ride only on trails designated for bicycles or in areas where you have the permission of the landowner.

- Be courteous to hikers or horseback riders on the trail, they have the right of way.

- Leave riding trails in the condition you found them. Be sensitive to the environment. Properly dispose of your trash. If you open a gate, close it behind you.

- Don't carry items or attach anything to your bicycle that might hinder your vision or control.

- Don't wear anything that restricts your hearing.

- Don't carry extra clothing where it can hang down and jam in a wheel.

Explanation of Symbols

ROUTES

▬▬▬▬	Biking Trail
■ ■ ■ ■	Bikeway
▬■▬■▬	Alternate Bike Trail
• • • • • •	Undeveloped Trail
■ ▬ ■ ■	Alternate Use Trail
= = = =	Planned Trail
▬▬▬▬	Roadway

FACILITIES

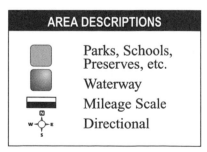

🔧	Bike Repair
⛺	Camping
➕	First Aid
❓	Info
🛏	Lodging
P	Parking
⛱	Picnic
🍴	Refreshments
🚻	Restrooms
🏠	Shelter
⛲	Water
MF	Multi Facilities

Refreshments   First Aid
Telephone   Picnic
Restrooms   Lodging

TRAIL USES

🚵	Mountain Biking
🚴	Leisure Biking
🛼	In Line Skating
🎿	Cross-Country Skiing
🚶	Hiking
🐴	Horseback Riding
🏔	Snowmobiling
🏍	All Terrain Vehicles

ROAD RELATED SYMBOLS

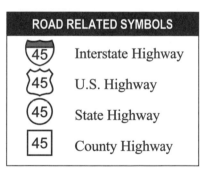

45	Interstate Highway
45	U.S. Highway
45	State Highway
45	County Highway

AREA DESCRIPTIONS

▢	Parks, Schools, Preserves, etc.
▢	Waterway
▬	Mileage Scale
✛	Directional

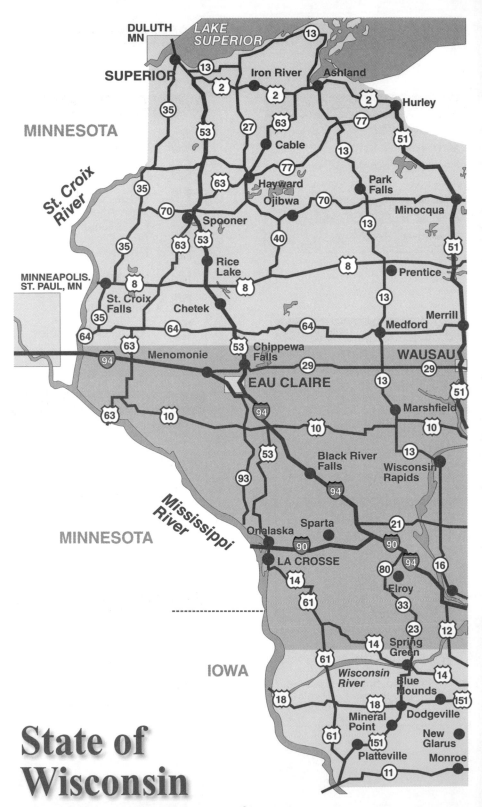

State of Wisconsin

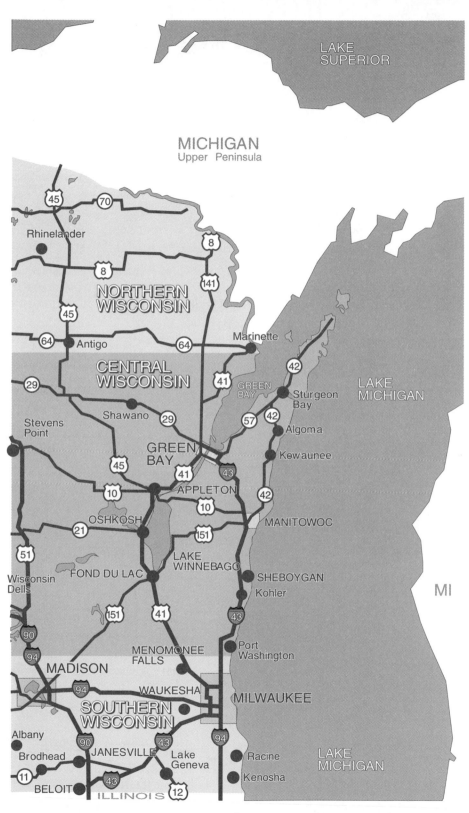

LAKE SUPERIOR

MICHIGAN
Upper Peninsula

Rhinelander

NORTHERN WISCONSIN

Antigo

Marinette

CENTRAL WISCONSIN

GREEN BAY

Sturgeon Bay

LAKE MICHIGAN

Shawano

Algoma

Stevens Point

Kewaunee

GREEN BAY

APPLETON

OSHKOSH

MANITOWOC

Wisconsin Dells

LAKE WINNEBAGO

FOND DU LAC

SHEBOYGAN
Kohler

MI

MENOMONEE FALLS

Port Washington

MADISON

WAUKESHA

MILWAUKEE

SOUTHERN WISCONSIN

Albany

Brodhead

JANESVILLE

Lake Geneva

Racine

LAKE MICHIGAN

Kenosha

BELOIT

ILLINOIS

9

Southern Section Overview

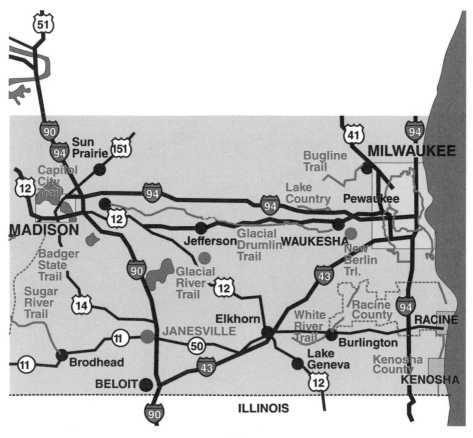

Central Section Overview

Northern Section Overview

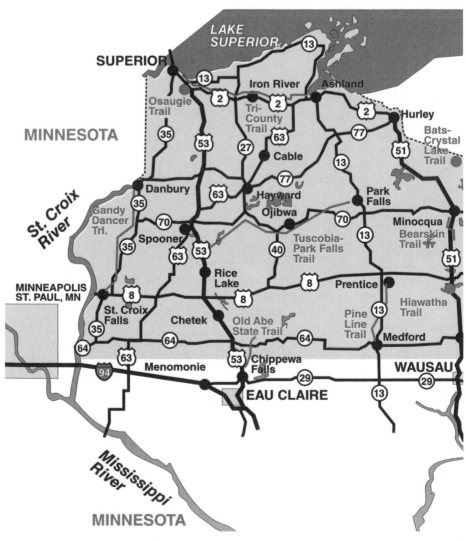

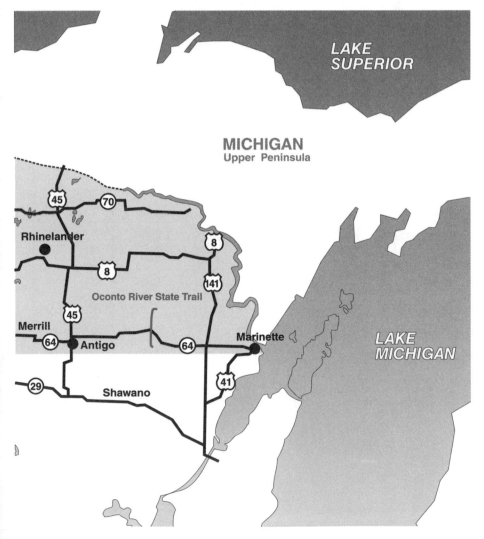

Mileage between Principal Cities

CITY	Appleton	Eau Claire	Green Bay	LaCrosse	Madison	Milwaukee
Appleton		173	30	167	103	102
Ashland	254	170	246	257	298	357
Beloit	148	225	185	182	47	78
Chicago, IL	189	307	201	283	144	90
Dubuque, IA	201	216	234	129	96	172
Duluth, Mn	324	153	317	244	329	389
Eau Claire	173		207	86	176	234
Fond Du Lac	40	189	62	165	71	63
Green Bay	30	207		206	137	117
Hayward	282	110	272	195	280	347
LaCrosse	167	86	206		142	198
Madison	103	176	137	142		77
Marinette	82	217	54	245	183	169
Milwaukee	102	234	117	200	77	
Racine	126	258	136	232	95	24
Rhinelander	141	150	129	238	203	231
Sheboygan	62	229	61	193	108	54
Stevens Point	66	107	92	116	107	154
Wausau	103	101	96	147	141	188
Wisconsin Dells	107	121	130	87	53	113

Bicycle Federation of Wisconsin

The Bicycle Federation of Wisconsin (BFW) Is a statewide membership-based nonprofit bicycle education and advocacy organization. Our mission, to make Wisconsin a better place to bicycle, embraces the basic vision behind our organization; that bicycling is a viable, healthy and environmentally sustainable means of transportation, recreation and sport. BFW provides bicyclists of all ages with information on recreational rides, safety tips and commuting skills. In addition, BFW educates decision makers, motorists, and bicyclists to the transportation and safety issues and environmental, health, and economic benefits of bicycling. We promote bicycling as an integral part of a balanced transportation system, a healthy and fun lifestyle, and a prosperous economy.

Specifically, the bicycle federation of Wisconsin's goals include:

* Promote effective bicycle education, encouragement and enforcement.

* Promote bicycling as a healthy, life-long activity.

* Promote bicycle-friendly policies and projects within state agencies, regional transportation areas, and local units of government.

* Promote motor vehicle driver education, awareness, respect, and safe interaction with bicyclists.

* Protect, defend and promote the legal rights of bicyclists.

* Provide a network of support, information and coordination for bicycle advocacy organizations, clubs, event organizers, and dealers throughout the state.

* Promote bicycle-friendly legislation within the state legislature.

For more information about the bicycle federation of wisconsin, or to become a member, visit their web site at: www..bfw.org, or call 608/251-4456. Your support makes what we do possible.

Enjoy bicycling and enjoy Wisconsin's trails!

Marjorie Ward
Executive Director, Bicycle Federation of Wisconsin

400 Trail

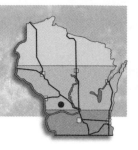

Length	27.5 miles
Surface	Limestone screenings
Location & Setting	The '400' Trail is a converted Chicago-Northeastern rail line running from Elroy to Reedsburg. The 27.5 mile trail, which includes a 5 mile spur from Union Center to Hillsboro, connects with the Elroy-Sparta and Omaha Trail in Elroy. The trail parallels the Baraboo River and crosses it 8 times. A 7.5 miles horse trail parallels the trail between Wonewoc and La Valle. Canoe launching sites are located along the Baraboo River. The countryside consists of scenic rolling hills, with deep, beautiful valleys, wooded hillsides, farms and quaint country roads.
Getting There	Reedsburg to Mirror Lake State Park: Take Hwy 23/33 to the 23 exit, then Hwy 23 to Shady Lane Road, and then to Hastings Road. The Park entrance is near the intersection of Hastings and Fern Dell Road.
Information	Wildcat Mountain State Park 608/337-4775 **www.reeds.com/trail**
County	Walworth

Area Overview

Galesville · 53 · 71 · 94 · 21 · 21
GREAT RIVER TRAIL · 27 · Tomah · Camp Douglas
Sparta · 90
ELROY-SPARTA TRAIL · OMAHA TRAIL · 51
16 · LA CROSSE RIVER TRAIL · 71
La Crosse · Cashton · 94 · 90 · 82
14 · 33 · Hillsboro · Elroy · 12
Stoddard · 27 · 131 · "400" TRAIL · 33 · Wisconsin Dells
MN · 56 · Viroqua · 80 · 58 · Reedsburg · 33 · Baraboo
IA · 82 · 51
35 · Richland Center · 12
171 · 14 · 90
61 · 80 · 94
27 · Wisconsin River · 14 · Madison
35 · WI
Prairie Du Chien · TO CHICAGO

18

Elroy is a city of some 1,600 people, and once was a prominent railroad center. It is the hub of three bike trails – Elroy-Sparta, '400', and Omaha. The trails meet at the Commons, a downtown park. The Commons provides parking, restrooms, lockers, showers, phone information, and picnic facilities.

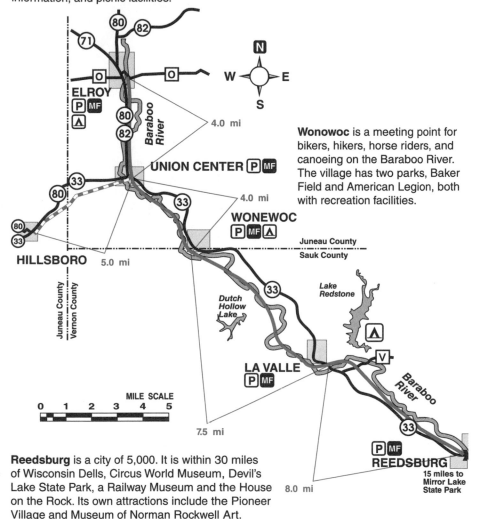

Wonowoc is a meeting point for bikers, hikers, horse riders, and canoeing on the Baraboo River. The village has two parks, Baker Field and American Legion, both with recreation facilities.

Reedsburg is a city of 5,000. It is within 30 miles of Wisconsin Dells, Circus World Museum, Devil's Lake State Park, a Railway Museum and the House on the Rock. Its own attractions include the Pioneer Village and Museum of Norman Rockwell Art.

Museum of Norman Rockwell Art - Almost 4,000 of the original magazine covers, story illustrations, advertisements and other memorabilia are on display. Norman Rockwell died in 1958 and is known as the "artist of the people". Open daily – year round. Located in Reedsburg at 227 S. Park Street.

Mid-Continent Railway - Experience a Steam Train ride from the early 1900's. Four trips daily from mid-May to Labor Day and on weekends until mid-October. Located in North Freedom.

Pioneer Log Village and Museum - Log library, log church, 3 log houses, blacksmith shop, country school and store, and 3 museum buildings. Located at Hwy 23 & 33, 3 miles east of Reedsburg. Open weekends from Memorial Day weekend through September. Donations only.

Model Railroad Museum - Operating Layouts with thousands of models on display near the Wisconsin Dells.

Ahnapee State Trail

Length	32 miles one way
Surface	Limestone screenings
Location & Setting	The Ahnapee State Trail is located in east central Wisconsin. The trail travels through several legs on abandoned railroad bed – from Algoma to Sturgeon Bay, and from Algoma to Casco Junction. Effort level is easy. Setting is farms, woods and marshland. A few sections of the trail are on public streets.
Getting There	The trailhead in Sturgeon Bay is located in Sawyer Park. There is on-street parking on Perry Street in Algoma, and on Hwy 54 in Casco.
Information	Door County Airport & Parks 920/746-9959 Friends of the Ahnapee 920/487-2041 Door County Chamber of Commerce 920/743-4456
County	**www.ahnapeetrail.org** Door, Kewaunee

STURGEON BAY

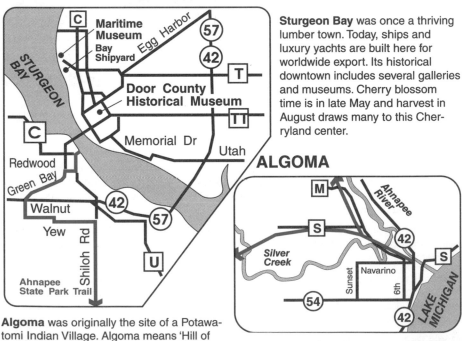

Sturgeon Bay was once a thriving lumber town. Today, ships and luxury yachts are built here for worldwide export. Its historical downtown includes several galleries and museums. Cherry blossom time is in late May and harvest in August draws many to this Cherryland center.

Algoma was originally the site of a Potawatomi Indian Village. Algoma means 'Hill of flowers'. The Stiehl Winery in downtown provides guided tours & tasting.

Ahnapee State Trail From lakefront Algoma, follow Hwy 42 to Cty 'S', then one mile west to Cty 'M', then ¾ miles to the Ahnapee State Trail. Watch for signs.

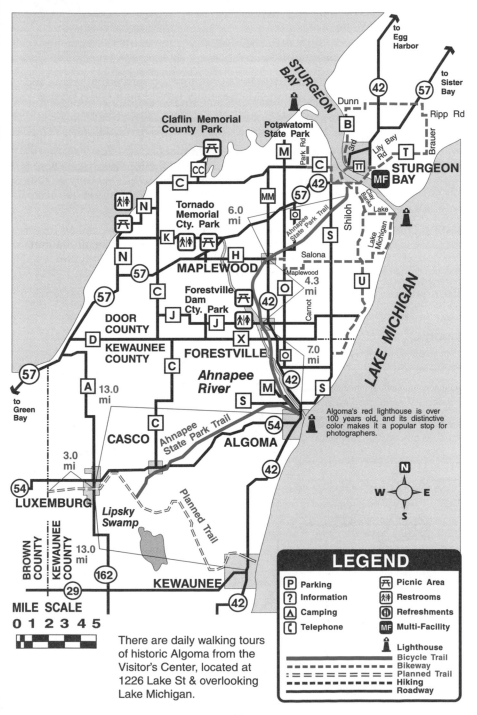

to
Egg
Harbor

to
Sister
Bay

Dunn

Ripp Rd

STURGEON BAY

Claflin Memorial
County Park

Potawatomi
State Park

Park Rd

3rd

Lily
Rd Bay

Brauer

**STURGEON
BAY**

Tornado
Memorial
Cty. Park

6.0
mi

MM

Ahnapee
State Park Trail

Clay
Banks

Shiloh

Lake

Lake
Michigan

MAPLEWOOD

Forestville
Dam
Cty. Park

Salona

Maplewood

4.3
mi

Carnot

DOOR
COUNTY

KEWAUNEE
COUNTY

FORESTVILLE

7.0
mi

to
Green
Bay

13.0
mi

*Ahnapee
River*

Algoma's red lighthouse is over
100 years old, and its distinctive
color makes it a popular stop for
photographers.

CASCO

Ahnapee
State Park Trail

ALGOMA

3.0
mi

LUXEMBURG

*Lipsky
Swamp*

Planned Trail

LAKE MICHIGAN

N
W • E
S

BROWN
COUNTY

KEWAUNEE
COUNTY

13.0
mi

KEWAUNEE

MILE SCALE

0 1 2 3 4 5

There are daily walking tours
of historic Algoma from the
Visitor's Center, located at
1226 Lake St & overlooking
Lake Michigan.

LEGEND

P Parking		🔼 Picnic Area	
? Information		🚻 Restrooms	
A Camping		Ⓡ Refreshments	
C Telephone		**MF** Multi-Facility	

Lighthouse
━━━━━ Bicycle Trail
━ ━ ━ ━ Bikeway
═ ═ ═ ═ Planned Trail
━━━━━ Hiking
━━━━━ Roadway

Badger State Trail

Length	40 miles
Location & Setting	This is a planned 40 mile trail, built on former rail grade, and extending from the Madison city limits south to the Illinois State line. The trail corridor passes through the cities of Fitchburg, Belleville, Monticello, and Monroe. It will intersect with the Capitol City State Trail in the city of Fitchburg, the Sugar River State Trail near Monticello, the Cheese Country Trail in the city of Monroe and also the Ice Age Trail. There is a tunnel between Belleville and Monticello. Presently only the 4 mile 'Southwest Path' within the city of Madison has been completed.
Getting There	The north trailhead is on North Randall Avenue and on Regent Street. It proceeds southwest past the Camp Randall Stadium, Glenwood Park, and Arrowhead Park to the intersection with the Capital City State Trails.
Information	Wisconsin Dept. of Natural Resources 608/275-3214
	www.dnr.state.wi.us/org/land/parks
County	Dane, Green

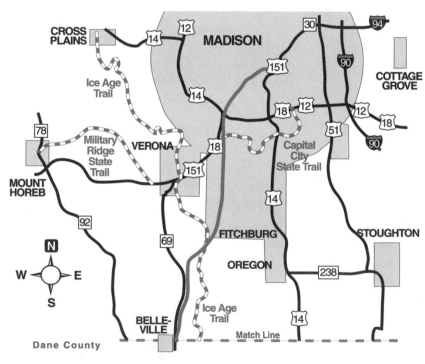

22

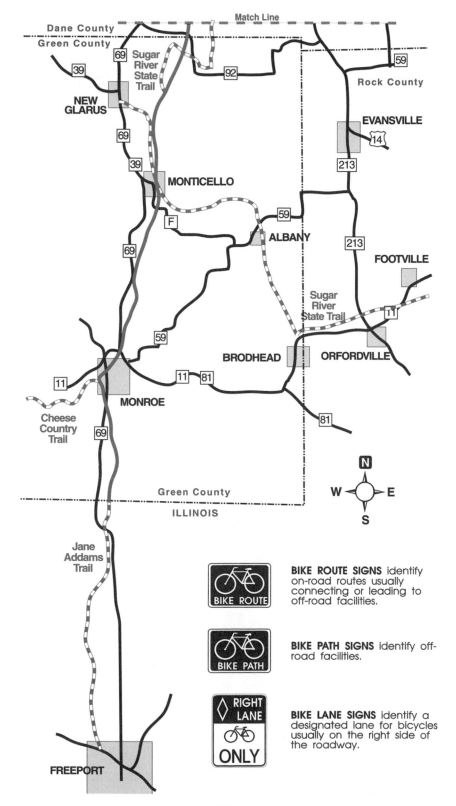

Match Line

Dane County
Green County

69 Sugar
River
State
Trail

39

NEW
GLARUS

92

59

Rock County

EVANSVILLE

14

69

39

MONTICELLO

213

F

59

69

ALBANY

213

FOOTVILLE

Sugar
River
State Trail

11

59

BRODHEAD

ORFORDVILLE

11

11 81

MONROE

Cheese
Country
Trail

81

69

N

Green County

W E

ILLINOIS

S

Jane
Addams
Trail

BIKE ROUTE SIGNS identify
on-road routes usually
connecting or leading to
off-road facilities.

BIKE ROUTE

BIKE PATH SIGNS identify off-
road facilities.

BIKE PATH

◇ RIGHT
LANE

ONLY

BIKE LANE SIGNS identify a
designated lane for bicycles
usually on the right side of
the roadway.

FREEPORT

BATS-Crystal Lake Trail

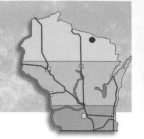

Length 11 miles one way

Surface Asphalt

Location & Setting Located in the Northern Highland-American Legion State Forest in far-north central Wisconsin, with Boulder Junction (known as the Musky Capitol of the World) as its northern trailhead. The setting is gently rolling through natural terrain, with several short, relatively steep sections. It passes in and out of pine, oak and maple forest as it parallels County M. Water, restroom and camping facilities are located near the trailheads and on the east side of Trout Lake. A state trail sticker is required. There are more than 1,300 lakes in Vilas County, the highest concentration of freshwater lakes in the world. There is a swimming beach at Crystal Lake.

Getting There Take Hwy 51 north out of Minocqua to County M. Continue northeast of Cty M for two miles to Cty N. East on Cty N for two miles take you to the southern trail, located at the Crystal Lake Campground. The northern trailhead is located just east of Boulder Junction off Cty K.

Information Boulder Junction Chamber of Commerce   715/385-2400

www.boulderjct.com

County Vilas

24

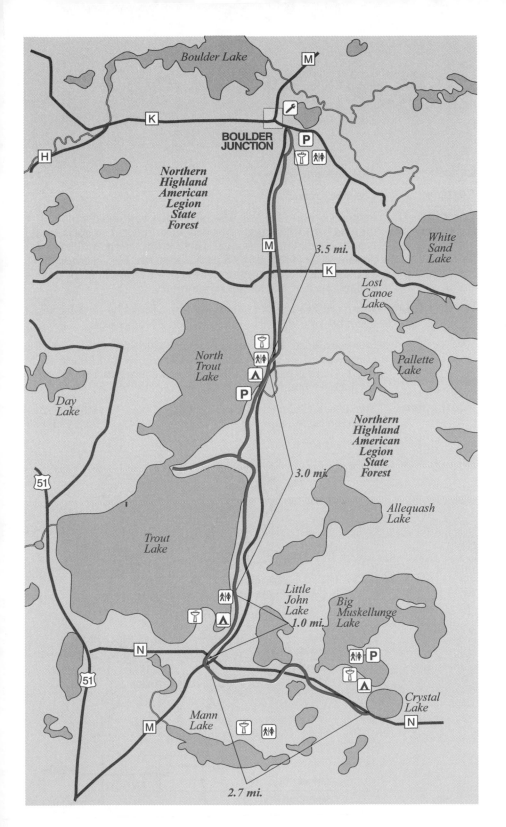

Bearskin State Trail

Length	18.3 mile one way
Surface	Crushed granite
Location & Setting	Located in north central Wisconsin, and built on abandoned railroad line. It's named after Bearskin Creek. The north trailhead is located in Minocqua, where information, trail passes, parking, food, lodging, and picnic areas are readily available. The surface is crushed granite. There are several campgrounds and resorts near the length of the route.
Getting There	North trailhead: Exit Hwy 51 on Front Street by the Minocqua Chamber of Commerce, and proceed 2 blocks west.
	South trailhead: Located on the north side of Hwy K, some 12 miles west of Rhinelander and a half mile west of Lakewood Road. There is parking at the trailhead and water a short distance beyond.

Information   Tomahawk Chamber of Commerce   800/569-2160
                    Bearskin State Trail   715/453-1263

                    www.wiparks.net

County   Price, Taylor

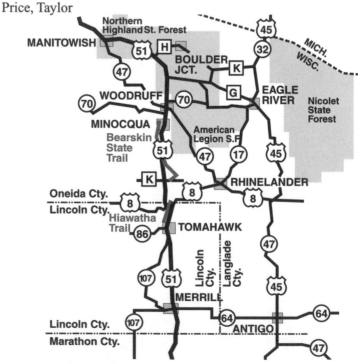

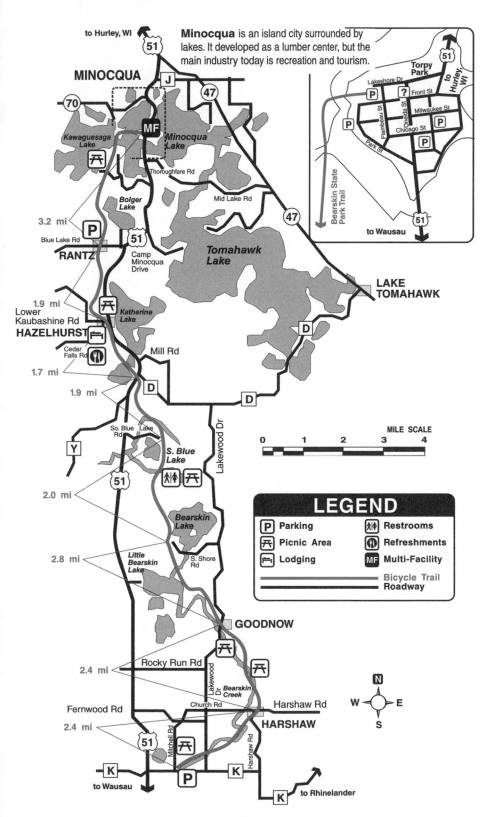

MINOCQUA is an island city surrounded by lakes. It developed as a lumber center, but the main industry today is recreation and tourism.

to Hurley, WI

MINOCQUA

Torpy Park

Lakeshore Dr

Front St

Milwaukee St

Flambeau St

Oneida St

Chicago St

Park St

to Hurley, WI

to Wausau

Bearskin State Park Trail

Kawaguesaga Lake

Minocqua Lake

Thoroughfare Rd

Bolger Lake

Mid Lake Rd

3.2 mi

Blue Lake Rd

RANTZ

Camp Minocqua Drive

Tomahawk Lake

LAKE TOMAHAWK

1.9 mi

Lower Kaubashine Rd

Katherine Lake

HAZELHURST

Cedar Falls Rd

Mill Rd

1.7 mi

1.9 mi

So. Blue Lake Rd

S. Blue Lake

Lakewood Dr

MILE SCALE

0   1   2   3   4

2.0 mi

Bearskin Lake

2.8 mi

Little Bearskin Lake

S. Shore Rd

LEGEND

P	Parking	🚻	Restrooms
🛆	Picnic Area	🏪	Refreshments
🛏	Lodging	MF	Multi-Facility

Bicycle Trail
Roadway

GOODNOW

Rocky Run Rd

2.4 mi

Lakewood Dr

Bearskin Creek

Fernwood Rd

Church Rd

Harshaw Rd

2.4 mi

Mitchell Rd

Harshaw Rd

HARSHAW

N
W — E
S

to Wausau

to Rhinelander

Buffalo River State Trail

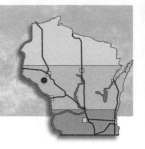

Length	36.4 miles one way
Surface	Fine gravel & cinder (the eastern portion is sandier)
Location & Setting	This multi-use trail is built on converted railbed and follows the Buffalo River between Mondovi and Fairchild in west central Wisconsin. The setting is open area, farmland, woods, hills, and small communities.
Getting There	Access the west trailhead by exiting south onto Marten Road at the intersection of Hwy 37 and Hwy 10. Parking with restaurants and lodging is a short distance away on hwy 10.
	The east trailhead is on Hwy 12 and 27 at the intersection of Hwy YY, about 1.5 miles north of Hwy 10. Access the trail from Fairchild by going west from the parking lot.
	In Eleva, enter the trail off Hwy 93 between Hwy 10 and the river. There is parking on the shoulder and a store nearby.
	The trail crosses Hwy D in the middle of Strum. There is a picnic area with restrooms at the intersection of Hwy D and the river.
	The trail cross Hwy 10 as you enter from the west of Osseo. There is a selection of food and lodging facilities at the nearby junction of Hwy 94 and 10.
Information	Buffalo River State Trail 608/534-6409
County	Buffalo, Trempealeau, Jackson

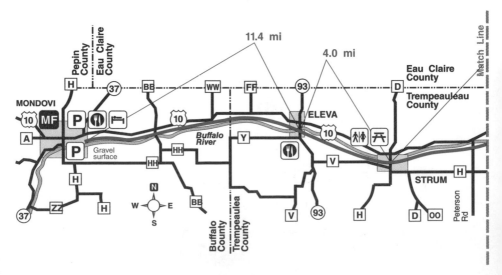

28

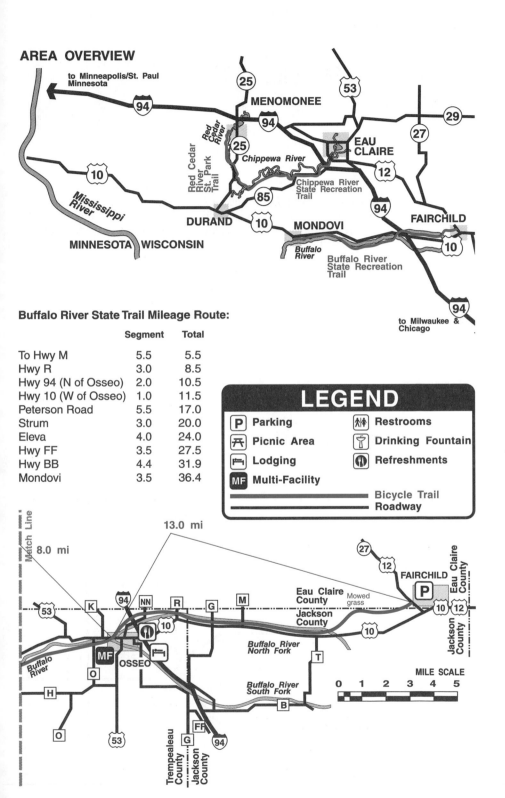

Bugline
Recreational Trail

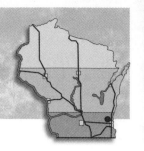

Length	12.2 miles one way
Surface	Crushed limestone
Location & Setting	This 12 mile trail was built on old railroad right-of way, and runs between Menomonee Falls and Merton. There is a separate parallel trail for horseback riding between 'The Ranch' outside of Menomonee Falls and Menomonee Park, plus additional bridle paths in Menomonee Park. There are 4.5 miles open to snowmobiling on the eastern section of the trail. Along the route you'll have an overview of one of the active Lannon Stone quarry pits. Dense woods hug much of the trail. Be aware that there are several busy road crossings on the eastern end.
Getting There	Located in southeast Wisconsin, the east trailhead is off Appleton Avenue just north of Hwy 175 in Menomonee Falls. The west trailhead is at the small village of Merton off Main Street (Cty KE) and south of Cty VV.
Information	Waukesha County Parks 262/548-7790 Waukesha Visitors Bureau 800/366-1961 **www.waukeeshacounty.gov/parks/trails/bike**
County	Waukesha

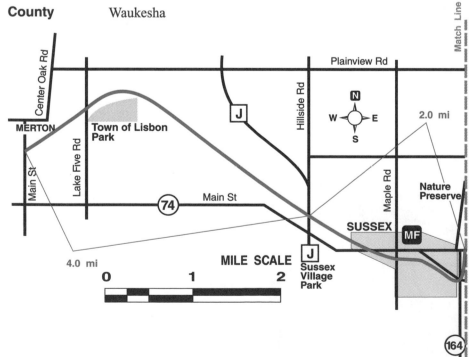

Menomonee Park 🎿⛷

Part of the Waukesha County Parks System, is a trailhead as well as a recreation site along the Bugline Trail. Facilities and activities include parking, restrooms, water, picnicking, camping, swimming, fishing, and sledding. Concessions are available at the beach house during the swimming season.

Length   Menomonee Park Hiking Trail 4.5 miles

Surface   Natural-groomed, wood chips

Setting   Wooded, rolling hills, wetlands

LEGEND

P	Parking	🚻	Restrooms
⛩	Picnic Area	🍴	Refreshments
?	Information	💧	Water
MF	Multi-Facility	**+**	First Aid
		▬▬▬	Bicycle Trail
		▬▬▬	Roadway

31

Capital City Trail

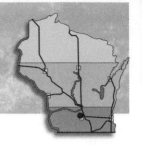

Length	18 miles
Surface	Asphalt
Location & Setting	The Capital City Trail was developed on a combination of green spaces and converted railbed. The trail breaks down to the 6.3 miles for the City of Madison section, 11.5 miles for the Nine Springs E way section, and 3.7 miles on the Military Ridge State Trail connection to the Cty PD trailhead. Spur trails lead to the University of Wisconsin Campus, the UW Arboretum and the Henry Vilas Zoo. Riding east from the Dahle Conservancy Park Trailhead in Fitchburg, the trail overlooks Dunn's Marsh. After crossing Seminole Hwy, you'll pass through stretches of oak and hickory woods, with some steep grades and through twisting creek bottom with three bridge crossings. The trail finally wraps around the north end of Lake Monona to where it currently ends at Hwy 51.
Getting There	There is a trailhead near the west end of Dahle Conservancy Park on Seminole Hwy, one mile south of the Hwy 12/14/18/151 interchange. Other trailheads are at Olin-Turville Park on John Nolan Drive, one mile north of Hwy 12/18; on Moorland Road 1.2 miles south of the Hwy 12/18 and South Towne Road interchange; downtown Madison at the Monona Terrace Park ramp on John Nole Drive/Hwy 151.

Information Greater Madison Visitors Bureau 800/373-6376
Dane County Parks 608/246-3896

www.visitmadison.com
www.co.dane.wi.us

County Dane

Madison is a bicycling town where bicycles outnumber autos. Bicyclists are assisted in their trails around central Madison by special bicycle related facilities with separate bicycle paths and lanes. Numerous bike racks are located throughout the area.

Bicycle registration is required in Madison and may be purchased at fire stations and bike shops. Dane County serves as the western trailhead of the Glacial Drumlin Trail and the eastern trailhead of the Military Ridge State Trail. There are also many roads throughout Dane County that are suitable for bike touring.

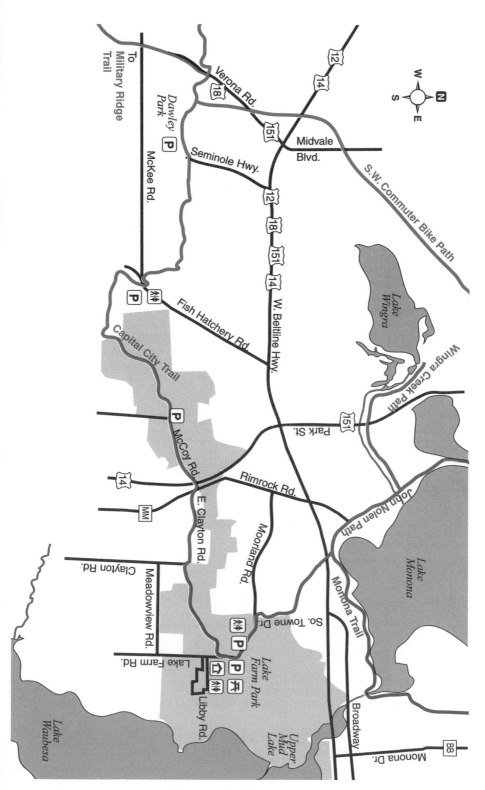

CE Trail

Length	4.2 miles one way
Surface	Asphalt
Location & Setting	The CE Trail is a corridor linking the Outagamie County cities of Appleton and Kaukauna. The trail parallels the north side of Cty CE between Hwy 441 in Appleton and Hwy 55 in Kaukauna. The surface is asphalt and 10 feet wide. It's part of a regional Greenway Corridor concept eventually linking the Mountain-Bay and Wiowash trails, and High Cliff State Park.
Getting There	The west trailhead is located on the north side of Cty CE at hwy 441.
Information	Outagamie County Planning 920/832-5255 www.co.outagamie.wi.us
County	Outagamie

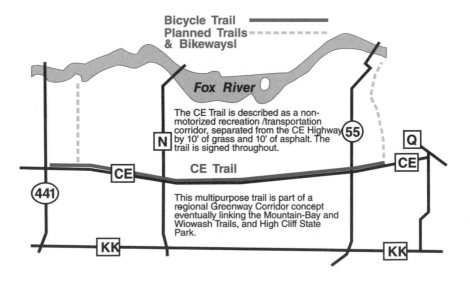

The CE Trail is described as a non-motorized recreation/transportation corridor, separated from the CE Hwy by 10 foot of grass and 10 foot of asphalt. The trail is signed throughout.

This multipurpose trail is part of a regional Greenway Corridor concept eventually linking the Mountain-Bay and Wiowash Trails, and High Cliff State Park.

AREA OVERVIEW - Appleton to Kaukauna

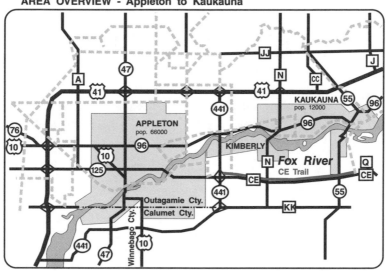

Cheese County Trail

LEGEND

🎪	Picnic Area	P	Parking
?	Information	🚻	Restrooms
🍴	Refreshments	🛏	Lodging
MF	Multi-Facility		

Bicycle Trail
Roadway
Alternate Trail

MINERAL POINT

P
39 MF
151
23
39
151
O

Mineral Point is the site of Pendavis and Shake Rag Valley where its early history is brought to life. It is also known for its cluster of artists and craftsmen.

Cheese Country Trail

Pecatonica River

23

O
O C
G
Pecatonica State Trail

CALAMINE

Cheese Country Trail
C
Pecatonica River
G
Bonner Branch
Pecatonica State Trail
G
Cheese Country Trail
Pecatonica River

9.0 mi **CALAMINE**

P 🚻
🎪 🍴
23
F

Darlington is the county seat of Lafayette County. There is a canoe festival in June. Their depot museum immortalizes the Milwaukee Road rail history of the area.

23
F
Pecatonica River
Vinegar Branch
23
81 **DARLINGTON**

Otter Creek

LAMONT 81

6.0 mi
J
DARLINGTON 81
81
P
MF 23
K
D
M
WIOTA
8 mi
176

GRATIOT

K
Pecatonica River
Wolf Creek
11
78
78
11
12 mi
K
78
Pecatonica River
GRATIOT
P 🚻
🎪 🍴
78
11
Cheese Country Trail

Match Line

Length	47 miles
Surface	Crushed stone
Location & Setting	This 47 mile one way trail is located in southwest Wisconsin. It parallels the Pecatonica River and was built on converted railroad right-of way. It connects with the Pecatonica Trail at Calamine. A 7 mile trail extension is planned between Belmont and Platteville. Tall prairie grass, majestic woods, river valleys and streams, wildflowers, wildlife, contoured fields and grazing farm animals are all part of the unforgettable views and adventures that await you. It passes through the communities of Browntown, South Wayne, Gratiot and Darlington, ending at Mineral Point. There are 57 overpasses, including a 449 foot bridge spanning the Pecatonica River south of Browntown.
Getting There	The east trailhead is in Monroe, which is six miles from the Illinois border, at 21st Street across from the Trail Park. The west trailhead is in Mineral Point at Jackson Street, east of Commerce Street.
Information	Pecatonica State Trail 608/523-4427 Monroe Chamber of Commerce 608/325-7648 **wicip.uwplatt.edu/green/ci/Monroe/outdoors/cc_trail**
County	Green, Iowa, Lafayette

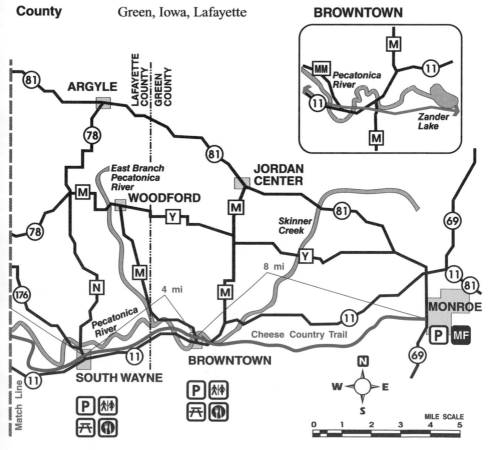

Chippewa River State Trail

Length	23 miles
Surface	Asphalt from Eau Claire to Hwy 85; Asphalt emulsion with pea-stone from Hwy 85 to Red Cedar Junction.
Location & Setting	The Chippewa River Trail is built on abandoned railbed and parallels the south side of the Chippewa River as it traces the quiet countryside between Eau Claire and the confluence of the Chippewa and Red Cedar Rivers. Your effort level will be easy. There are several museums, and a steam train in Carson Park as well as other historic sites in Eau Clair. Bike Rentals are also available. A State trail pass is required for those 16 and over. The Chippewa River was once the "Road of War" for the Ojibwe (Chippewa) and Dakota (Sioux). The conflict raged for more than 150 years with the last battle taking place near Eau Claire in 1854.
Getting There	The east trailhead is located in Carson Park, 1 mile north of Clairmont Avenue (Hwy 12) in Eau Claire. Another trailhead is at the wayside park on Hwy 85, 2.5 miles west of the I-94/Hwy 37/85 Eau Claire/Mondovi exit.
Information	Eau Claire Area Visitors Bureau 715/831-2345 **www.chippewa-river-trail.com**
County	Eau Claire, Dunn

Bike rentals are available. Other activities include canoeing and pontoon boating, with both rental and tours. Cross-country skiing is allowed in the city parks. There is automobile drag racing off Hwy 85 in Caryville.

Match Line

H

H

CARYVILLE

P

Red Cedar State Park Trail

Chippewa River

MERIDEAN   no public facilities

85

Chippewa River State Park Trail

O

6.0 mi

85   5.0 mi

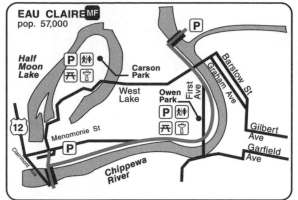

EAU CLAIRE MF
pop. 57,000

Half Moon Lake

P 🚻 🎋 🚰
Carson Park

West Lake

Owen Park
P 🚻
🎋 🚰

First Ave

Graham Ave

Barstow St

P

Gilbert Ave
Garfield Ave

12

Menomonie St

P

Claremont Ave

Chippewa River

Trail passes are required for bikers 16 year old and older. Passes are daily or annual, and are good on all Wisconsin State Trails.

Access to water, restrooms, and picnic areas are conveniently located along the Eau Claire trail extension. The city offers a complete selection of facilities and many points of interest.

The Wayside Rest Area on Hwy 85 between Eau Claire and Caryville has parking, restrooms, water, picnic area, and offers a beautiful view overlooking the Chippewa River.

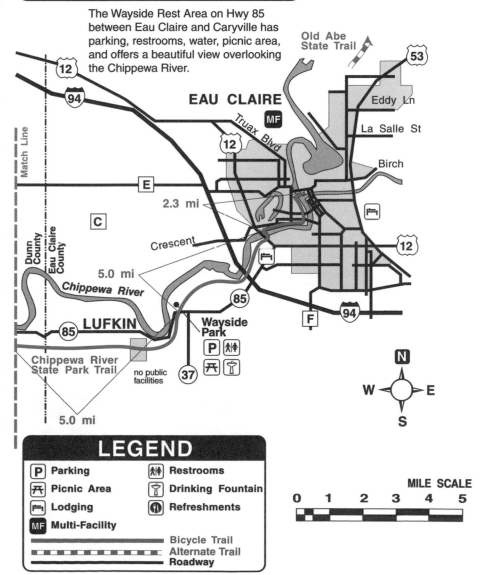

Door County Trails

Information   Door County Chamber of Commerce
920/743-4456

www.door.county.com
www.doorcounty-wi.com

MILE SCALE

0 1 2 3 4 5   10

Emergency Assistance - Dial 911

LEGEND

P	Parking	🎪	Picnic Area
?	Information	🚻	Restrooms
A	Camping	🍴	Refreshments
C	Telephone	MF	Multi-Facility
		🗼	Lighthouse

- - - - - - Bicycle Trail
- - - - - - Bikeway
- - - - - - Mtn. Biking
- - - - - - Hiking
————— Roadway

Peninsula State Park
Sunset & Hidden Bluff Trail

Length	5.8 miles (plus 7 miles of mountain biking trails)
Surface	Limestone screenings (except the mountain biking trails)
Location & Setting	The park has 3,763 acres of forest, dolomite cliffs, marsh, and meadows. Park roads are narrow and heavily traveled. Use of the Sunset Bike Trail and back roads is encouraged. Many of the roads have steep downgrades with corners and intersections. Ride single file, under full control, wear safety attire and be prepared to stop.
	A Wisconsin park sticker is required on all vehicles entering the park, and can be purchased at the park headquarters.
Information	Peninsula State Park 920/868-3258

www.wi.parks.net

The Eagle Bluff Lighthouse is on the National Register of The Park is located on the Green Bay side in upper Door County. From Sturgeon Bay, take Hwy 42 north past Egg Harbor to the park entrance.

Historic Places. Located in Peninsula State Park between Fish Creek and Ephraim. It was built in 1868 and has been restored.

The park's facilities include sand beach and bathing beach, numerous picnic areas, a nature center and several hundred campsites. Naturalist programs are conducted from June to September.

A visit to Eagle Bluff Lighthouse and a climb to Eagle tower will enhance your visit.

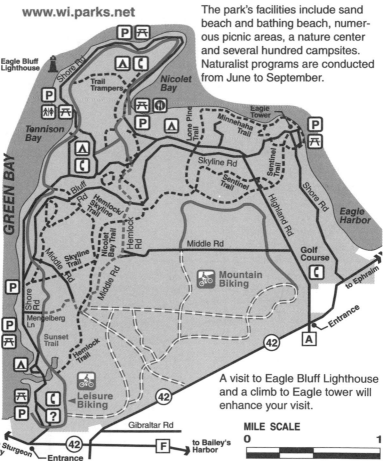

MILE SCALE
0   1

Elroy-Sparta State Trail

Length	32 miles
Surface	Limestone screenings
Location & Setting	This 34 mile one way trail was established in 1965, and was the first rails-to trails conversion in the country, and is also one of the most popular. The entire corridor is a wildlife refuge. There are three tunnels, with the longest between Sparta and Norwalk at more than three-quarters of a mile long. Walking through the tunnels (don't ride) is an adventure in itself. The local scenery includes bluffs, valleys, and friendly small towns. Sparta is the connecting point to the north end of the Elroy-Sparta trail and the east end of the LaCrosse River Bike Trail. Elroy serves as the connecting point to the east end of the Elroy-Sparta Trail, the south end of the Omaha Trail and the north end of the '400' Trail. A State trail pass is required.
Getting There	East Trailhead (Elroy): From Hwy 90/94, exit at Hwy 12/16 northwest for 12 miles to Hwy O, then west on Hwy O for 15 miles to Elroy. West Trailhead (Sparta): From the east exit Hwy 90 at Route 16 and proceed west for 3 miles.

Sparta is known as the 'Bicycling Capitol of America'.

Facilities available at the Sparta depot include parking, restrooms, water, information and telephone.

Wildcat Mountain State Park is located 8 miles south of the trail via Hwy T or 131. The 3,500 acre park provides picnic areas, a seven mile cross-Country ski trail, hiking, and horse trails. Highlights include canoeing on the Kickapoo River and the scenery at Observation Point.

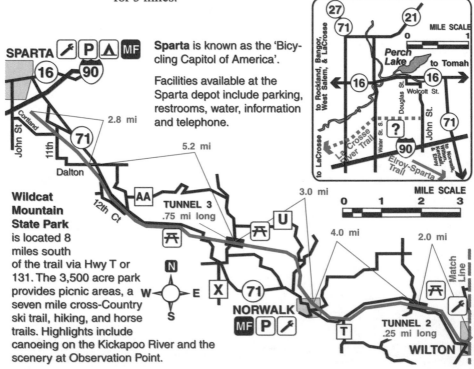

Information

Sparta Visitors Bureau   800/354-2453
Elroy-Sparta State Trail Headquarters   608/463-7109
www.elroy-sparta-trail.org

County   Monroe, Juneau

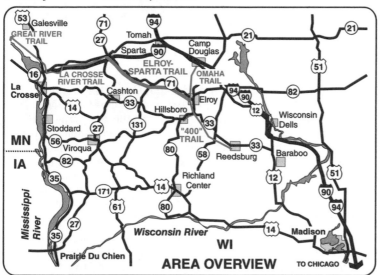

AREA OVERVIEW

ROUTE SLIP	INTERVAL	TOTAL
Elroy (Trailhead)	3.5	3.5
33rd	2.5	6.0
Kendall	3.0*	9.0
Tunnel #1 (.25m)	2.5	11.5
27th St.	3.5	15.0
Wilton	2.0*	17.0
Tunnel #2 (.25m)	4.0	21.0
Norwalk	3.0*	24.0
Tunnel #3 (.75m)	5.2	29.2
Dalton Ave.	2.8	32.0
Sparta (Trailhead)		

*To Tunnel midpoint

LEGEND

🛆 Picnic Area	🅿 Parking
? Information	🚻 Restrooms
🍷 Refreshments	🛏 Lodging
🔧 Bicycle Service	🅰 Camping

MF **Multi-Facilities Available:**

Picnic Area	Restrooms	Refreshments
Water	Phone	Lodging

▬▬▬ Bicycle Trail
━━━ Roadway

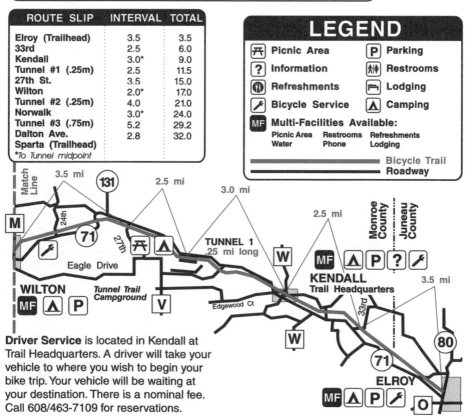

Driver Service is located in Kendall at Trail Headquarters. A driver will take your vehicle to where you wish to begin your bike trip. Your vehicle will be waiting at your destination. There is a nominal fee. Call 608/463-7109 for reservations.

Fox River State Trail

Length	13.5 miles
Surface	Asphalt and crushed limestone
Location & Setting	The trail follows the Fox River through Green Bay, Allouez and DePere before heading to the tiny village of Greenleaf. The northern 6.5 miles are asphalt-paved, and the southern 7 miles are crushed limestone. There are scenic boat landings and parks along the city portion. The northern trailhead lies in the heart of downtown Green Bay, with many restaurants and other service close at hand. Attractions include the Children's Museum, National Railroad Museum, Green Bay Packer Hall of Fame, the new zoo near Suamico, and the Bay Beach Amusement Park at the mouth of the Fox River. A trail pass is required.
Getting There	The northern trailhead is at the intersection of East Mason Street (Hwy 29) and Adams Street in Green Bay. The southern trailhead is in Greenleaf off Hwy 96 just east of Hwy 57.
Information	Packer Country Regional Tourism Office 920/494-9507, 800/867-3342
	Brown Country Park District 920/448-6242
	www.packercountry.org **www.foxrivertrail.org**
County	Brown

The Fox River State Trail

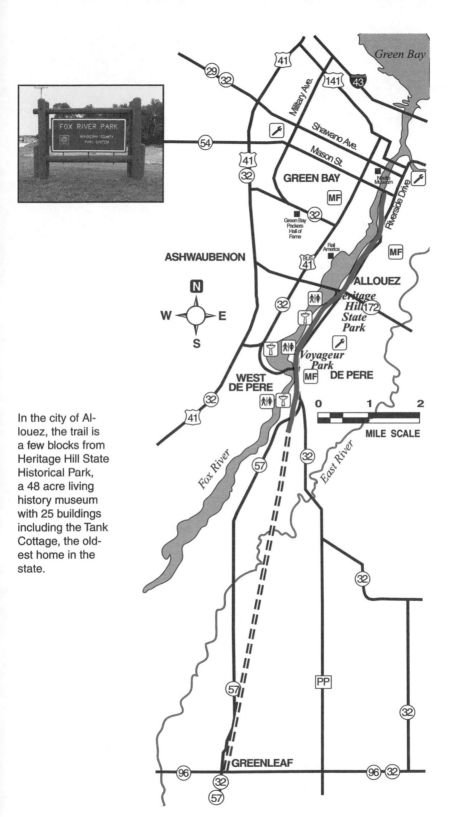

FOX RIVER PARK
WAUKESHA COUNTY
PARK SYSTEM

Green Bay

Military Ave.

Shawano Ave.

Mason St.

GREEN BAY

Naval
Museum

Riverside Drive

Green Bay
Packers
Hall of
Fame

Rail
America

ASHWAUBENON

ALLOUEZ

Heritage
Hill
State
Park

N

W ←○→ E

S

Voyageur
Park

WEST
DE PERE

DE PERE

0   1   2

MILE SCALE

In the city of Allouez, the trail is a few blocks from Heritage Hill State Historical Park, a 48 acre living history museum with 25 buildings including the Tank Cottage, the oldest home in the state.

Fox River

East River

PP

GREENLEAF

Friendship State Trail

Length	4 miles
Surface	Crushed limestone
Location & Setting	This 4 mile trail runs along the south side of Hwy 10 from the east side of Horn Park in Brillion to the small village of Forest Junction in east central Wisconsin. It was built on converted railbed. Brillion State Wildlife Area is located just south of the trail. There are plans to connect the Friendship Trail and the Fox River Trail.
Getting There	Forest Junction is about 15 miles east of the Appleton/Menesha area via Hwy 10.
Information	Calumet County Parks 920/439-1008
County	Calumet

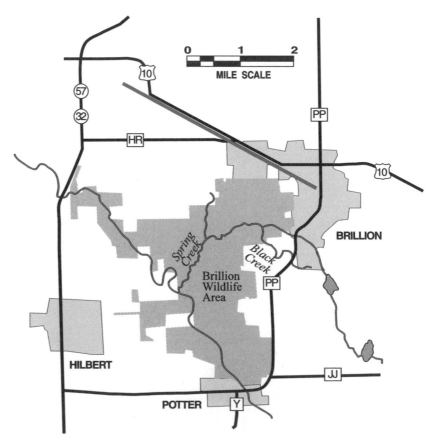

Glacial River Trail

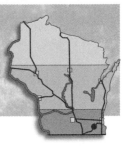

Length	6 miles
Surface	Asphalt, with limestone screenings near the south trailhead
Location & Setting	The Glacial River Trail was built on former railbed, and runs from Farmco Lane and Janesville Avenue at the south end of Fort Atkinson to the Rock County line. Between Farmco Lane and Groeler Road you'll cross an 80 foot wooden bridge over Allen Creek. The trail is asphalt paved to Koshkonong Lake Road, and then continues on crushed limestone to the Rock/Jefferson County line. You'll pass through a covered bridge on the trail about a mile from the county line. Parking lots are located at both the north and south trailheads.
Getting There	From For Atkinson, proceed on Janesville Avenue (Hwy 26) to Farmco Lane, then go right a short distance to the trailhead.
Information	Jefferson County Parks 920/674-7260 donnah@co.jefferson.wi.us
County	Jefferson

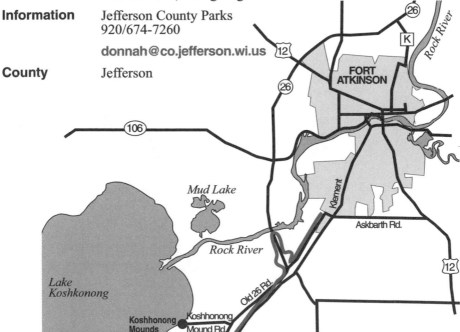

47

Gandy Dancer Trail

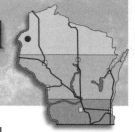

Length	48 miles surfaced, plus an additional trail in Minnesota (98 miles total)
Surface	Crushed limestone (remaining surface is railroad grade & mostly in Minnesota)
Location & Setting	A 98 mile trail with 48 miles surfaced with crushed limestone between St. Croix Falls and Danbury. From Danbury, the remaining 50 miles of trail continues north through Minnesota on exiting railroad grade and ends back in Superior, Wisconsin. The setting is rural, small town, and agricultural, with many scenic vistas of lakes, rivers, and forest. It was developed on abandoned railbed. The distances between the towns along the trail are never more than 10 miles apart. The entire trail is marked with mile post signs. There are also park and rest areas along the route. The Gandy Dancer Trail was named for the railroad workers who used tools from the Gandy Tool Company. State trail use passes are required of anyone 16 years of age or older, and are available in the towns at selected vendors along the trail.

Getting There The south trailhead and trail headquarters is located at the Polk County Information Center, located on the east side of Hwy 35 South, south of Hwy 8.

Information Polk County Tourism 800/222-7655

Burnett County Tourism 800/788-3164 715/349-7411

Douglas County Forestry Dept. 715/378-2219

www.burnettcounty. com/tourism/trail

www.wiparks.net

County Polk, Burnett, Douglas

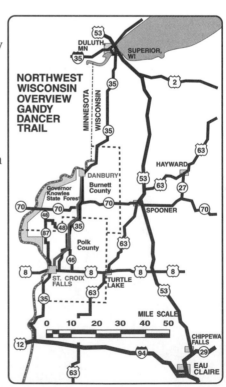

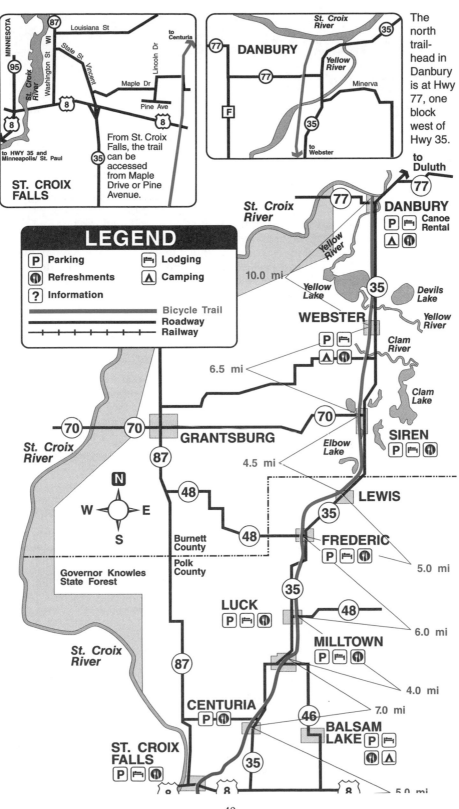

ST. CROIX FALLS

MINNESOTA
WI

87
Louisiana St
to Centuria
State St
Washington St
Vincent
Lincoln Dr
95
St. Croix River
Maple Dr
Pine Ave
8
8
35
8
to HWY 35 and
Minneapolis/ St. Paul

From St. Croix Falls, the trail can be accessed from Maple Drive or Pine Avenue.

DANBURY

St. Croix River
77
Yellow River
77
Minerva
F
35
to Webster

The north trail-head in Danbury is at Hwy 77, one block west of Hwy 35.

to Duluth
77

St. Croix River
77
DANBURY
P ⌂ Canoe Rental
A (M)

Yellow River
10.0 mi
Yellow Lake
35
Devils Lake
WEBSTER
Yellow River

LEGEND

P Parking
⌂ Lodging
(M) Refreshments
A Camping
? Information

Bicycle Trail
Roadway
Railway

P ⌂
A (M)
6.5 mi

Clam River

Clam Lake

70
70
GRANTSBURG
70
SIREN
P ⌂ (M)

St. Croix River
87
Elbow Lake
4.5 mi

N
48
W E
S
48
48
LEWIS
35
FREDERIC
P ⌂ (M)

Burnett County
Polk County
5.0 mi

Governor Knowles State Forest

35
LUCK
P ⌂ (M)
48
6.0 mi

MILLTOWN
P ⌂ (M)
4.0 mi

87
CENTURIA
P (M)
46
7.0 mi

ST. CROIX FALLS
P ⌂ (M)
35
BALSAM LAKE
P ⌂
(M) A

8
8
5.0 mi

49

Glacial Drumlin State Trail

Length	52 miles
Surface	Limestone screenings, 13 miles paved nearest Waukesha
Location & Setting	The Glacial Drumlin State Park Trail runs from Waukesha, by the Fox River Sanctuary, to Cottage Grove, 13 miles east of Madison. The trail was built on abandoned rail line and passes through many small communities, prairie remnants, and farmland. It comes within a few miles of the Aztalan State Park, Lapham Peak, and the South Unit of Kettle Moraine State Forest. There is a trail connector to Sunset Park, a little west of Co Hwy TT and north of Sunset Dr. There is a 2 mile gap in the trail between Helenville and Jefferson requiring the use of low traffic road connections. Snowmobilers are not allowed on the paved section of the trail. A state trail use pass is required.

There are numerous accesses along its route. |
Getting There	The east trailhead: From I-94, exit Hwy 164 (North Street), south through 6 stoplights to St. Paul Avenue, then right to MacArthur Road. Take a right on MacArthur Road for ¼ mile to the Fox River Sanctuary, where you can pick up the trail.
Information	Glacial Drumlin Trail – East 262/646-3025 Glacial Drumlin Trail – West 920/648-8774 **www.glacialdrumlin.com** **www.wiparks.net**
County	Waukesha, Jefferson, Dane

Western Section

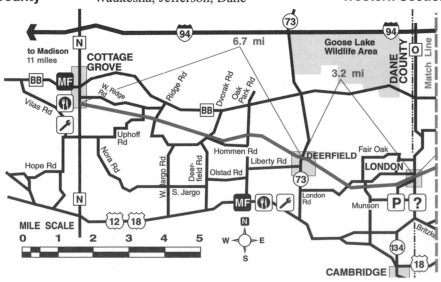

50

GLACIAL DRUMLIN STATE TRAIL OVERVIEW

ST. CROIX FALLS

From St. Croix Falls, the trail can be accessed from Maple Drive or Pine Avenue.

Deerfield
Trail is located on Hwy 73 on the north edge of downtown. Facilities include restaurants and bicycle service. Drumlins are the long hills left behind by melting glaciers thousands of years ago.

East-West Trail Connection
Coming from the east, take Cty 'Y' south ¼ mile to Junction Road, then west 1.5 miles to where the trail picks up again heading northwest (about .2 miles east of Hwy 26).

Lake Mills Trailhead
Take Hwy 90 to Cty 'A' train depot station. There is parking at the trail. Services include restaurants and village parks with water and restrooms.

Portions of the trail between Cty 'O' and 'S' may be closed at times during the summer for herbicide application.

GLACIAL DRUMLIN STATE PARK TRAIL ROUTE SLIP:		
Waukesha	SEGMENT	TOTAL
Wales	6.5	6.5
Dousman	4.5	11.0
Sullivan	6.6	17.6
Helenville	5.9	23.5
Switzke Rd.	2.1	25.6
East-West Connection	*4.0 mi. bikeway*	
Lake Mills	5.9	31.5
London	5.8	37.3
Deerfield	3.2	40.5
Cottage Grove	6.7	47.2

Western Section

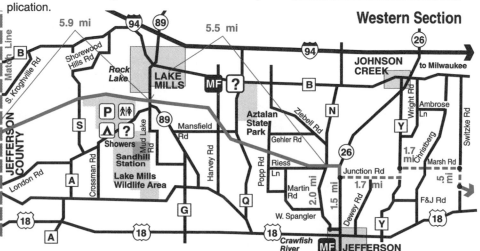

51

Glacial Drumlin State Trail (continued)

Eastern Section

LEGEND

P	Parking	水	Restrooms
⛺	Picnic Area	?	Information
🍴	Refreshments	A	Camping
🔧	Bicycle Service	MF	Multi-Facility

━━━ Bicycle Trail
▬ ▬ ▬ Bikeway
━━━ Roadway

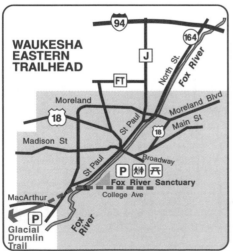

Sullivan Trailhead
Take Hwy 18 west from Cty 'F' to Palmyra Street and the trail crossing. Parking and restrooms are adjacent to the trail on Palmyra Street. Facilities include restaurant, village park, picnicking.

Dousman Trailhead
Take Hwy 18 west of Hwy 67 to Main Street. Go south on Main Street ¾ mile to the trail crossing. Parking is adjacent to the trail. Service includes restaurants, and a village park next to the trail with water and restrooms.

You can camp at the Kettle Moraine and Lake Kegonsa State Parks, and at the Nagawicka County Park. The trail crosses the Rock and the Crawfish rivers. Many area lakes provide fishing and boating opportunities.

Eastern Section

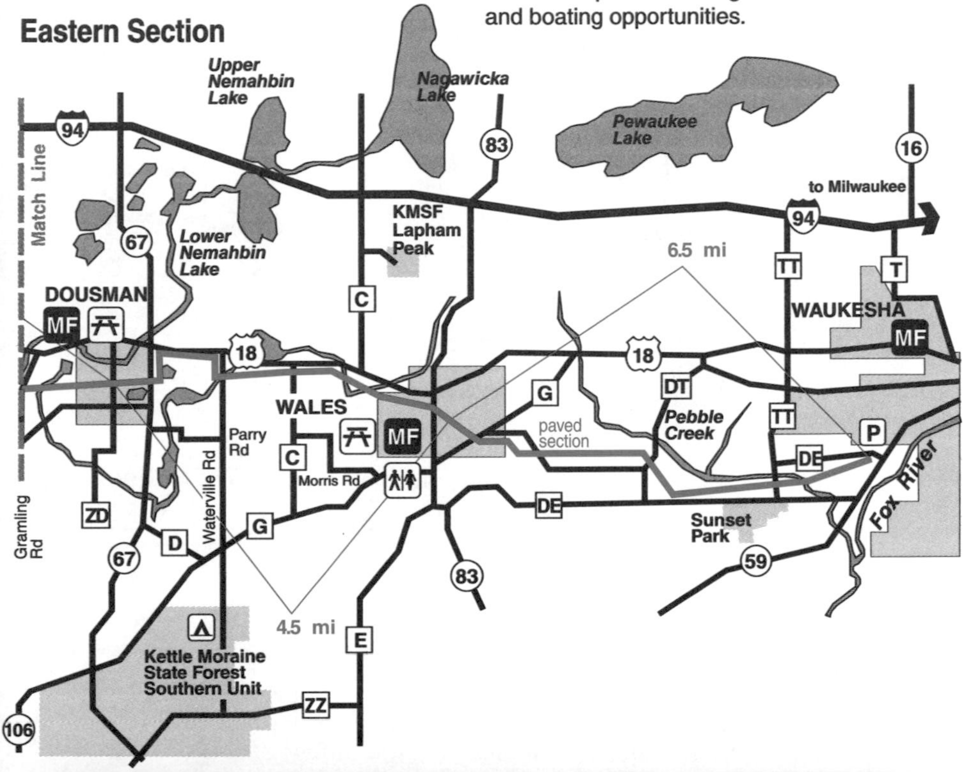

Upper Nemahbin Lake

Nagawicka Lake

Pewaukee Lake

94

83

16

to Milwaukee

67

Lower Nemahbin Lake

KMSF Lapham Peak

6.5 mi

94

TT

T

Match Line

DOUSMAN

MF

C

WAUKESHA

MF

18

18

G

DT

Pebble Creek

WALES

MF

paved section

TT

P

Parry Rd

C

DE

Waterville Rd

Morris Rd

DE

ZD

G

Sunset Park

59

Gramling Rd

67

D

83

4.5 mi

E

Kettle Moraine State Forest Southern Unit

ZZ

106

Fox River

The Glacial Drumlin State Trail

Great River State Trail

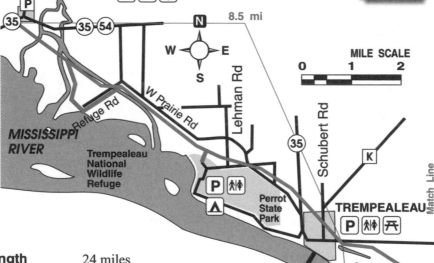

MARSHLAND

MISSISSIPPI RIVER

Trempealeau National Wildlife Refuge

Perrot State Park

TREMPEALEAU

Lock & Dam 6

Trempealeau Wildlife Area

8.5 mi

10.75 mi

MILE SCALE
0   1   2

Refuge Rd · W Prairie Rd · Lehman Rd · Schubert Rd

Length	24 miles
Surface	Limestone screenings
Location & Setting	Located near LaCrosse, the trail runs from Onalaska northwest through Trempealeau, and by Perrot State Park and the Trempeleau National Wildlife Refuge, to Hwy 54/35 just south of Marshland. It was established in 1967, and built on abandoned Chicago and Northwestern railroad bed. Enjoy the beauty of the Mississippi River with its majestic limestone bluffs and surrounding countryside as you travel the trail. There are 18 bridges along its length. State Trail use passes are required.
Getting There	East trailhead: Medary, ½ mile east of the Hwy 16 and Cty B intersection.
	Northwest trailhead: From Hwy 35 near Marshland, take Wildlife Refuge Road east of the tracks.
	The Onalaska trailhead is located at Hilltopper and Oak Forest Drive. Exit Hwy 35N off I-90.
Information	Perrot State Park 608/534-6409
	Center for Tourism 800/873-1901
	www.wi.parks.net
County	LaCrosse, Trempealeau

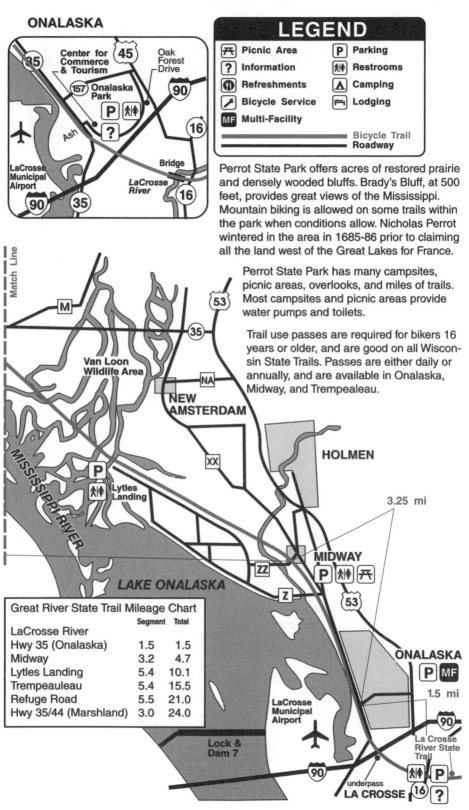

ONALASKA

LEGEND

🎪 Picnic Area		P Parking	
? Information		🕴 Restrooms	
🍴 Refreshments		⛺ Camping	
🔧 Bicycle Service		🛏 Lodging	
MF Multi-Facility			

━━━ Bicycle Trail
━━━ Roadway

Perrot State Park offers acres of restored prairie and densely wooded bluffs. Brady's Bluff, at 500 feet, provides great views of the Mississippi. Mountain biking is allowed on some trails within the park when conditions allow. Nicholas Perrot wintered in the area in 1685-86 prior to claiming all the land west of the Great Lakes for France.

Perrot State Park has many campsites, picnic areas, overlooks, and miles of trails. Most campsites and picnic areas provide water pumps and toilets.

Trail use passes are required for bikers 16 years or older, and are good on all Wisconsin State Trails. Passes are either daily or annually, and are available in Onalaska, Midway, and Trempealeau.

Match Line

Van Loon Wildlife Area

NEW AMSTERDAM

HOLMEN

3.25 mi

Lytles Landing

MIDWAY

LAKE ONALASKA

ONALASKA

1.5 mi

LaCrosse Municipal Airport

Lock & Dam 7

La Crosse River State Trail

underpass
LA CROSSE

Great River State Trail Mileage Chart

	Segment	Total
LaCrosse River		
Hwy 35 (Onalaska)	1.5	1.5
Midway	3.2	4.7
Lytles Landing	5.4	10.1
Trempeauleau	5.4	15.5
Refuge Road	5.5	21.0
Hwy 35/44 (Marshland)	3.0	24.0

Green Circle Trail

Length	30.5 miles
Surface	Asphalt, crushed graniye, wood chipps
Location & Setting	The Green Circle Trail consists of 14 segments, totaling over 30 miles. The setting is greenway and urban. The trail surface varies from crushed granite, to asphalt, streets and wood chips. Much of the trail system parallels the Wisconsin and Plover Rivers and they flow through the communities and then join. The 14 mile Tomorrow River State Trail connects at Hoover Road, just north of Porter Road.
Information	Portage County Parks Dept 715/346-1433
	www.altrails.com/rail/wi/sevenspoint.htm
County	Portage

Segments & Directions

A. Riverfront 2.5 miles. Trail starts near Bank One where Hwy 10 crosses the Wisconsin River, and goes north through Bukolt Park. Park at Bukolt or near the Bank One/Chamber lots.

B. Stagecoach 2.0 miles

C. Holiday 1.0 miles. Start at either the southeast corner of the Zenoff Softball Park or off Northpoint Drive about one block west of the Holiday Inn.

D. University 2.5 miles. Can be accessed on the south side of North Point Drive, across from Schmeeckle Reserve Visitor Center on Northpoint Drive about a block east of Michigan Avenue. The trail loops University Lake.

E. Moses Creek 2.5 miles

F. Plover River 4.0 miles. You can access at the east end of Barbara's Lane (Go east on Hwy 10 to Green Avenue in Park Ridge. Turn north to Jordan Lane, and then east on Janick Circle which become Barbara's Lane), or east on Hwy 66 past the airport and Torun Road to the Ski Lodge just past the Izaak Walton entrance on the south side of Hwy 66.

G. Iverson Park 2.5 miles. Loops from the parking lot in Iverson Park at the foot of Hillcrest Drive (Jefferson Street). Go to Park Ridge on Hwy 10 East, turn south on Sunrise Avenue to Hillcrest Drive, then turn east through the gateway downhill to the parking lot.

H. McDill 1.5 miles. Start at Hwy HH one block east of Feitz Avenue, or at Heffron Street Between Feitz Avenue and Leahy Avenue, or Patch Street just east of the bridge.

I. Whiting Park 1.5 miles. Access near the traffic light corner of McDill Road (Hwy HH) and Post Road (Business 51), or turn west off Post road on Cedar Street to the dead end.

J. Paper Mill 1.5 miles

K. River Pines 2.0 miles. Starts from the western parking lot of Stevens Point Nursing/Rehab Center and parallels the river to the City Wastewater Plant at the west end of Bliss Avenue (Parking). It continues up to Bliss Avenue, to Tomarack, to Wisconsin, to Water Street, and to Bank One.

L. Hoover Road 4.0 miles. From Hwy 10 East, turn south at the traffic light on Country Club Drive. Proceed about a mile to Ponderosa Street where the trail begins.

M. Westside Loop 2.5 miles.

N. Mainland Meadows .5 miles.

Stevens Point

LEGEND

🎪 Picnic Area	🅿 Parking		
❓ Information	⛺ Camping		

Bicycle Trail
Bikeway
Roadway

57

Hiawatha Bike Trail

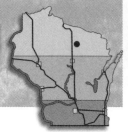

Length 6.6 miles

Surface Rotten granite screenings

Location & Setting The Hiawatha Trail is built on abandoned Milwaukee Road railroad bed, and goes north from Tomahawk to the Lincoln County line near Lake Nokomis. It is operated by Lincoln County. There are numerous private campgrounds, hotels, and resorts in the area. The trail's name commemorates the famous poem by Henry Wadsworth Longfellow, "The Song of Hiawatha".

Getting There From the junction of Hwy 51 and 86 in Tomahawk, proceed west on Somo Avenue to the Sara Park Activity Center, which serves at the south trailhead.

Information Tomahawk Chamber of Commerce   715/453-5334
Lincoln County Forestry and Parks   715/536-0327
www.co.lincoln.wi.us

County Lincoln

Oneida County
Lincoln County

Deer Lake

Public Beach

Crystal Lk.

Lake Nokomis

Half Moon Lake

Clear Lake

1.5 mi

Bus. 51   2.3 mi

Nibler Rd.

Muskellunge Lake Rd.

.9 mi

Norten Rd.

Bus. 51   Mohawk Dr.   1.9 mi

Sara Park Activity Center
W. Somo Ave

TOMAHAWK

E. Somo Ave

Bus. 51

to Merrill & Wausau

MILE SCALE
0   1   2

N
W   E
S

There are plans for extending the trail two miles north of the Lincoln/Oneida County line, and eventually linking it to the Bearskin State Trail to the north.

There is no admission charge for the Hiawatha Trail.

58

Hillsboro State Trail

Length	4.3 miles
Surface	Limestone screenings
Location & Setting	The Hillsboro Trail is a spur off the '400' Trail, which in turn connects to the Elroy-Sparta and Omaha Trails. The countryside consists of scenic rolling hills, with deep valleys, wooded hillsides, and farms. Hillsboro calls itself the Czech Capital of Wisconsin.
Getting There	The east trailhead connects with the '400' Trail in Union Center, near the intersection of Cty 33 and Cty 80/82. Hillsboro is about 9 miles south of Elroy on Cty 80/82.
Information	Wildcat Work Unit 608/337-4775 Hillsboro City Park 608/489-2350
County	**www.wiparks.net**

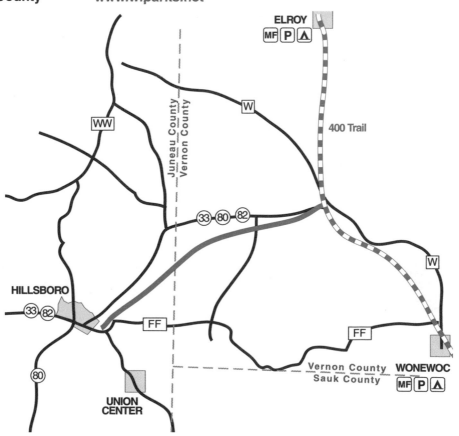

Janesville Area Trails

Length & Surface

Kiwanis Trail 1.5 miles mile paved from Dawson Field to Centerway.
Street segment from Rockport Road to Kiwanis Trail
1.5 mile gravel trail from Kiwanis Trail north

Rock Trail 1.3 mile paved from Dawson Field to Afton Road
0.3 miles on Afton Road
2.6 mile gravel trail from Boat Launch south

Springbrook Trail 4.8 mile paved trail connecting downtown Janesville to Rotary Gardens., Palmer Park, the Youth Sports Complex and Hwy 14

Hwy. 11 Bypass Trail is a 2.1 mile paved trail from Afton Road to Center Avenue

Location & Setting

Janesville is the southernmost access point to the Ice Age Trail, and has 14 miles of trail within the city limits. When the last glacier to cover Wisconsin began to recede, the southern extent pushed long ridges of glacial material between Janesville and Milton forming a boundary known as the Terminal. The trail setting is urban and parkways. The economy is manufacturing and agriculture.

Getting There

Janesville is located in south central Wisconsin at the junction of Hwy 90 and Hwy 50.

Information

Janesville Leisure Services Division	608/755-3030
Janesville Visitors Bureau	608/757-3171

leisure@ci.janesville.wi.us
www.janesvillecvb.com

County

Rock

Janesville is named after Henry F. Janes, who arrived in 1836 and built a small cabin on the banks of the Rock River. By 1860, Janesville had 10,000 residents and was the second largest city in the state at that time. Janesville has seven historic Districts of homes and buildings listed on the National Register of Historic Places.

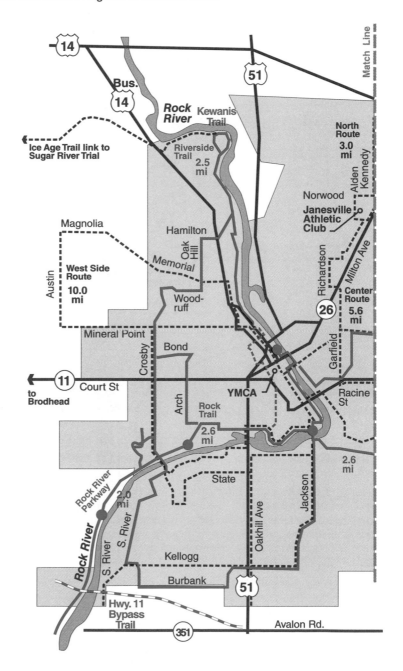

Janesville Area Trails (continued)

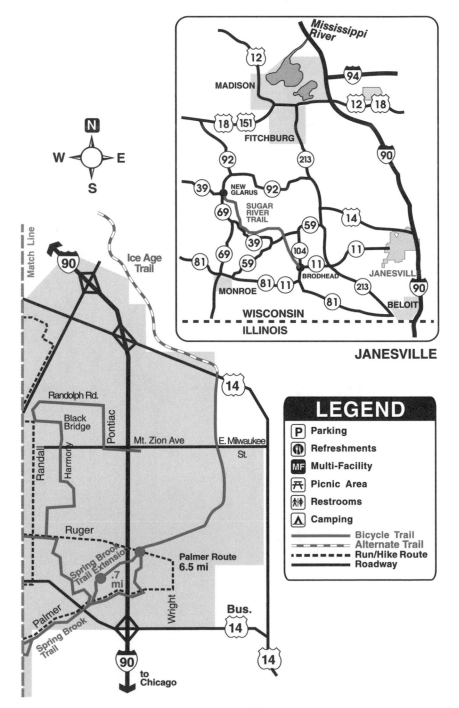

JANESVILLE

LEGEND

P	Parking
🛈	Refreshments
MF	Multi-Facility
🛆	Picnic Area
🚻	Restrooms
🛆	Camping

Bicycle Trail
Alternate Trail
Run/Hike Route
Roadway

Kenosha County Trail

Length	Pike Trail – 9.5 miles County Bike Trail – 9 miles
Surface	Pike Trail – paved with some on-street connections County Bike Trail – crushed limestone
Location & Setting	Your ride will take you through open areas, sparse woods, and urban streets. The Pike Bike Trail is a marked Trail. The 3.5 mile southern section links with the south end of the County Bike Trail at 30th Avenue and 89th Street, and connects with the McClory Bike Path in Lake County, Illinois. The northern section of the Pike Trail links with the north end of the County Bike Trail at 35th Street and 27th Avenue, and connects to Racine's North Shore Trail. Restrooms and water are located along the lakefront parks. Kenosha highlights include the oldest operating velodrome (an oval track for bike racing) in the nation, opening in 1927, its lakefront beaches and parks, and three National Register Historic Districts.
Getting There	There are numerous access points throughout Kenosha's trail system through street connections and parkways.
Information	Kenosha Visitors Bureau 800/654-7307 Kenosha County Parks 262/857-1869 **www.kenoshacvb.com** **www.a1trails.com/rail/wi.kenosha**
County	Kenosha

Kenosha County Trail (continued)

Overview

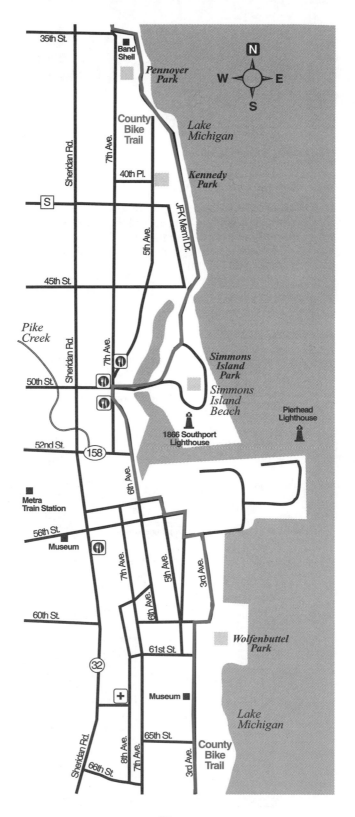

35th St.

Band Shell

Pennoyer Park

N
W E
S

County Bike Trail

Lake Michigan

7th Ave.

40th Pl.

Kennedy Park

Sheridan Rd.

JFK Mem'l Dr.

S

5th Ave.

45th St.

Pike Creek

Sheridan Rd.

7th Ave.

Simmons Island Park

Simmons Island Beach

50th St.

Pierhead Lighthouse

1866 Southport Lighthouse

52nd St.

158

6th Ave.

Metra Train Station

56th St.

Museum

7th Ave.

5th Ave.

3rd Ave.

60th St.

6th Ave.

Wolfenbuttel Park

61st St.

32

Museum

Lake Michigan

Sheridan Rd.

8th Ave.

7th Ave.

65th St.

3rd Ave.

County Bike Trail

66th St.

65

LaCrosse River Trail

Length	21.5 miles
Surface	Limestone screenings
Location & Setting	The trail parallels the LaCrosse River and is a connecting link between the Elroy-Sparta and the Great River Trails. It was developed from the abandoned Chicago and Northwestern Railroad between Sparta and Medary Junction, just outside of LaCrosse. Farmlands, wooded hillsides, trout streams and Neshonoc Lake adorn the trail. The terrain is flat. Campground and public parks are located in or near the communities adjoining the trail. Bridges along the trail have planked floors and railings in place for your safety.

LaCrosse sits on the convergence of three rivers: the LaCrosse River, the Black River, and the Mississippi River. The area was first visited by Father Louis Hennepin in 1680. Permanent settlement began in 1841.

Match Line

Great River Trail

53

LAKE ONALASKA

Upper Mississippi River National Wildlife and Fish Refuge

35 Onalaska Park P

108

P WEST SALEM Lake Neshonoc

ONALASKA

157

LaCrosse Municipal Airport

90

16

OS

Veterans Memorial Park

La Crosse River

90

M

B

90

53

35

16

P ? MEDARY

MEDARY

7.0 mi

14 61

16

LA CROSSE

P

? Bicycle Service

16

26 Minnesota

14 Wisconsin

61

35 14

61

Upper Mississippi River National Wildlife and Fish Refuge

Center for Commerce & Tourism 45 Oak Forest Drive

35

157 Onalaska Park 90

P

Ash ?

16

LaCrosse Municipal Airport

Bridge

LaCrosse River 16

90 35

66

Getting There   The east trailhead is located in Sparta. From Hwy 90, proceed north for 2 miles on Rte 27, or west of 3 miles on Rte 16. The west trailhead is in Medary, off Hwy 16.

Information   Wildcat Mountain State Park   608/337-4775

www.lacrosseriverstatetrail.org

County   Monroe, LaCrosse

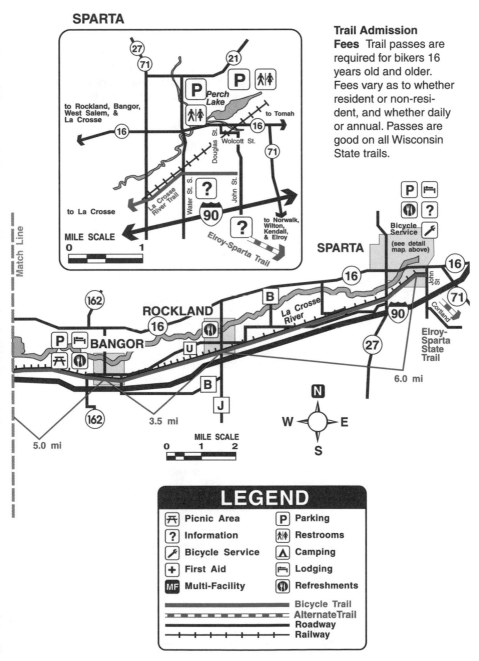

Trail Admission Fees Trail passes are required for bikers 16 years old and older. Fees vary as to whether resident or non-resident, and whether daily or annual. Passes are good on all Wisconsin State trails.

LEGEND

🎋	Picnic Area	P	Parking
?	Information	🚹🚺	Restrooms
🔧	Bicycle Service	△	Camping
+	First Aid	🛏	Lodging
MF	Multi-Facility	🍺	Refreshments

━━━━ Bicycle Trail
═══ AlternateTrail
━━━━ Roadway
┼┼┼┼ Railway

67

Lake Country Recreational Trail

Length	8 miles
Surface	Crushed limestone
Location & Setting	The trail utilizes the Wisconsin Electric Power Company's right-of way, which was also a former railroad bed. It has access to the Naga-Waukee Park just west of Hwy 83. This park has a vehicle entrance fee. The trail shares the road with vehicles for short distances at Cty SS and Oakton Road and at Wells Street in the city of Delafield.
Getting There	Located in southeast Wisconsin, between the Landsberg Center trailhead, just north of I-94 on Golf Road, and Cushing Park in the city of Delafield. The Lake Country Trail is accessible at all road crossings and at Naga-Waukee Park. Trail information, parking, shelter, and water are available at the Landsberg Center trailhead next to the Country Inn. Near the west end of the trail in Delafield is a selection of food shops and other facilities.
Information	Waukesha County Parks 262/548-7790
County	Waukesha

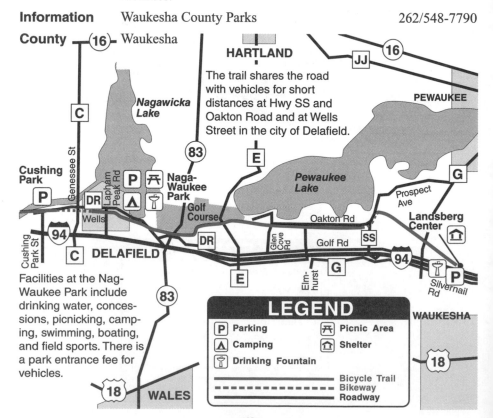

The trail shares the road with vehicles for short distances at Hwy SS and Oakton Road and at Wells Street in the city of Delafield.

Facilities at the Nag-Waukee Park include drinking water, concessions, picnicking, camping, swimming, boating, and field sports. There is a park entrance fee for vehicles.

LEGEND

P	Parking	**Picnic Area**	
A	Camping	**Shelter**	
Drinking Fountain			
	Bicycle Trail		
	Bikeway		
	Roadway		

The Bicycle Federation of Wisconsin

Bicycle Trails Don't Just Happen
by Michael D. Barrett

All of the trails highlighted in this book share in a common idea: The idea that a trail dedicated to human-powered mobility could bring a community together. To be sure, recreation, exercise, clean transportation, and environment all figure into the trail equation, but ultimately, community is what these trails are all about.

Many of the trails included here are abandoned rail corridors which have been converted into biking and hiking trails - commonly referred to as rail trails. All of the trails, whether rail trails, corridors in a park, or connectors between cul-de-sacs in subdivisions have succeeded beyond the dreams of even the most ardent supporters.

Communities along the trails are rightly proud of their trails. The trail is often a means to showcase the specialness of their place. But rail trails and other linear park trails did not just happen; they are the product of the imagination and dedication of civic-minded folks.

The idea of a rail-to-trail conversion has been around for a while, beginning with central Wisconsin's Elroy-Sparta Trail in the mid-1960's. However, the current network of hundreds of trail miles did not blossom until the 1990's. Why did it take so long to get going? Money.

Communities Take Charge

Though the success of the Elroy-Sparta trail in boosting local economies was well-known, the ability of other small towns to harness the funds for trails was limited...until the passage of the landmark 1991 Intermodal Surface Transportation Efficiency Act (ISTEA).

Before your eyes glaze over from the bureaucratese, here is a summation: Prior to the passage of ISTEA all federal transportation funds given over to local governments had to be spent on highways. With ISTEA, local governments could use a small percentage of their transportation funds on other modes, such as walking and biking. Trails flourished. Flexible transportation dollars meant that pent-up citizen demand for community-friendly biking and walking facilities could be met. The rapid expansion of "human power only" trails is the direct result of greater local control over transportation funds.

Bike Trails Under Fire

Local control over transportation money has come up against serious opposition in recent election cycles. Yet the discussion has nothing to do with budget cutting; it is a question of where the dollars will go, not how much will be spent. The transportation pie will stay the same size, whether ISTEA survives or not. Legislators from the major parties have stated that if there is enough citizen input for continued local control (for bike and pedestrian projects) under ISTEA, they will support it. So if you would like to see more of these trails, let your legislator know that ISTEA should continue, bicycle funding included.

Remember: Once these linear corridors - heirlooms of our railroading past and connections to our communities' future - are lost, they are gone forever.

(continued on page 83)

69

Mariners Trail

Length	12 miles
Surface	Paved
Location & Setting	This 12 mile asphalt-paved trail joins Manitowoc to Two-Rivers and Point Beach State Forest. It is open to bicyclists, in-line skaters and walkers. The Mariners Trail hugs the scenic shoreline of Lake Michigan, and provides the longest, continuous view of the Lake in the state of Wisconsin. Bike rentals are available in Two Rivers and Manitowoc. Additional accommodations in route include restaurants, picnic tables, viewing telescopes, beaches, and motels. Point Beach is home to the historic Rawley Point Lighthouse, towering 111 feet over the point. In Manitowoc you'll find the Wisconsin Maritime Museum and Lake Gardens, with its 6 acres of stunning formal gardens. The trail will eventually be extended into downtown Two Rivers.
Getting There	Manitowoc is located about 50 miles north of Milwaukee along Hwy 43 and the Lake Michigan shoreline. A good place to start is the Wisconsin maritime Museum. The trailhead is at the 8th Street Bridge. In Two Rivers, Neshotah Beach or the Lighthouse Inn serves as a good trailhead. Parking is available at all of these locations.
Information	Manitowoc Area Visitors Bureau 800/627-4896
	www.manitowoc.org/marinestrail/htm1
County	Manitowoc

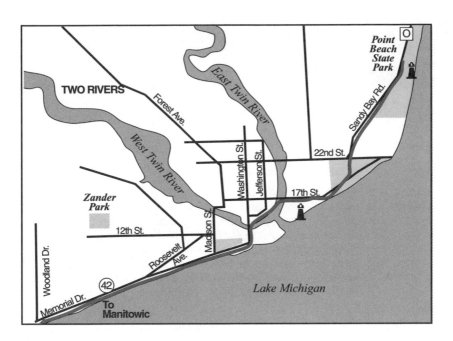

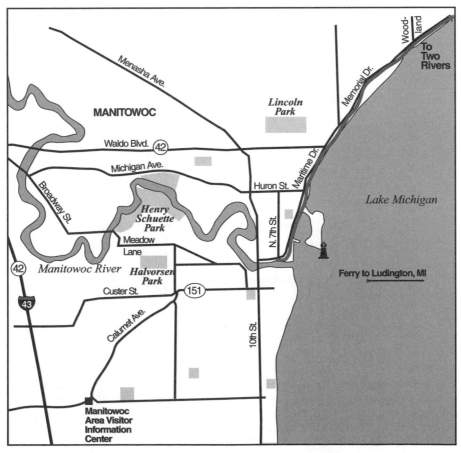

Mascoutin Valley State Trail

🚴 🏃 ⛷ 🎧 🏕

Length	31 miles
Surface	Limestone screenings
Location & Setting	The Mascoutin Valley State Trail is a 31 mile recreation trail extending from Fond du Lac to Berlin on former railroad line. The 9 mile Fond du Lac section and the 12 mile Ripon to Berlin section are surfaced with limestone screenings. The area is a mix of prairie and woods with extensive wetland and agricultural land near Rosendale. From Fond du Lac, the trail passes west through the 6,000 acre Eldorado Marsh. Food and drink is available in all the communities through which the trail passes.
Getting There	Fond du Lac is about 60 miles north of Milwaukee via Hwy 41. There is a trailhead with parking at Rolling Meadows Drive in Fond du Lac. In North Ripon there is a trailhead with parking adjacent to the trail on Locust Road north or Ripon. There is also a trailhead parking lot in Berlin.
Information	Fond du Lac County Parks 920/929-3135 Winnebago County Parks 920/232-1960 **areas.wildernet.com/pages/area**
County	Fond du Lac, Green Lake, Winnebago

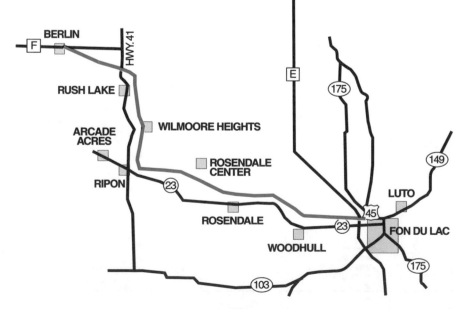

ROUTES

▬▬▬▬	Biking Trail
▬ ▬ ▬ ▬	Bikeway
▬▬▬▬	Alternate Bike Trail
• • • • • •	Undeveloped Trail
■ ■ ■ ■	Alternate Use Trail
= = = =	Planned Trail
▬▬▬▬	Roadway

FACILITIES

🔧	Bike Repair
⛺	Camping
➕	First Aid
?	Info
🛏	Lodging
P	Parking
⛱	Picnic
☕	Refreshments
🚻	Restrooms
🏠	Shelter
🚰	Water
MF	Multi Facilities

Refreshments   First Aid
Telephone   Picnic
Restrooms   Lodging

TRAIL USES

Mountain Biking

Leisure Biking

In Line Skating

Cross-Country Skiing

Hiking

Horseback Riding

Snowmobiling

All Terrain Vehicles

ROAD RELATED SYMBOLS

(45)	Interstate Highway
(45)	U.S. Highway
(45)	State Highway
45	County Highway

AREA DESCRIPTIONS

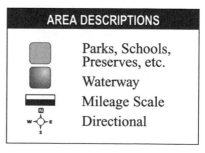

Parks, Schools, Preserves, etc.

Waterway

Mileage Scale

Directional

Military Ridge State Park Trail

Length	39.6 miles
Surface	Crushed limestone
Location & Setting	This trail runs between Madison and Dodgeville, following an old military road built in 1855. The surface is limestone screenings except for a 3 mile stretch between Madison and Verona. The setting consists of farmland, prairie, woodlands and wetlands. Between Verona and Mt. Horeb the trail climbs slowly from east to west, often on hillsides, through mostly agricultural landscapes. Between Mt. Horeb and Ridgeway the trail mostly parallels Hwy 151/18. Blue Mounds State Park, a little west of Blue Mounds, offers swimming and scenic overlooks. As a side excursion, take the trail connection to Governor Dodge State Park with its extensive recreation facilities.
Getting There	There is easy access to the trail from all the communities along the route. To get to the Verona trailhead, take the Cty PB exit of 151/18, and turn right at the end of the ramp (this is Nesbitt Road). You'll find the trailhead about a mile north on Nesbitt Road.
Information	Military Ridge State Park 608/437-7303
	www.wiparks.net
County	Dana, Iowa

Dodgeville Located at the gateway to the Uplands, a geographic maze of rolling farmlands, wooded valleys and rugged sandstone bluffs. Wildlife in the area includes fox, turkeys, deer and coyotes.

Trail Admission Fees Trail passes are required for bikers 16 years old and older. Fees vary as to whether daily or seasonal. Passes are good on all Wisconsin State Trails.

LEGEND

P	Parking	🚻	Restrooms
?	Information	🏕	Picnic Area
⛺	Camping	🛏	Lodging
🍴	Refreshments	+	First Aid
MF	Multi-Facility		
▬▬▬▬			Bicycle Trail
- - - -			Mountain Biking
▬▬▬▬			Roadway

Governor Dodge State Park Located 3 miles north of Dodgeville on Hwy 23. It is the 2nd largest state park in Wisconsin. The terrain in the park is rugged and varies from steep hills and sandstone bluffs to deep lush valleys. Activities include hiking, horseback riding, swimming, picnicking, and camping. There is an admission fee.

Cave of the Mounds Located 3 miles west of Mt. Horeb just off Hwy 18/151. A guided tour of the Cave takes you past a varied collection of stalactites, stalagmites, columns and other formations. There are park-like grounds with picnic areas, rock gardens and an outdoor amphitheater.

Little Norway Located 3 miles west of Mt. Horeb among the rolling hills of Blue Mounds. It is known as the "Valley of the Elves". The guides will tour you through buildings containing the largest privately owned collection of Norwegian antiques in the country.

Mount Horeb The "Troll" capitol of the world. The area is rocky with abrupt hills and narrow, winding valleys. Attractions include Cave of the Mounds, Little Norway, several small museums and a number of tourist shops.

Shuttle Service A driver will transport cyclists to a desired point along the Trail from Mt. Horeb and return your car to Mt. Horeb.

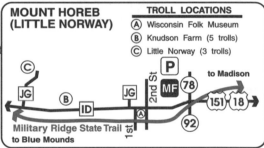

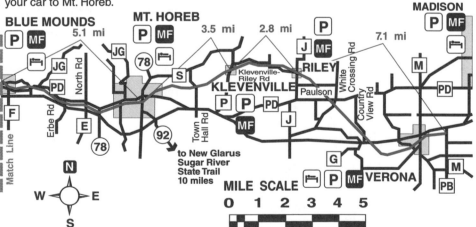

House on the Rock Wisconsin's number one attraction, and a place of mystery and intrigue. It was started in the early 1940's by Alex Jordan on a 60 foot chimney or rock. Exhibits include the Streets of Yesterday, the Music of Yesterday, the world's largest Carousel, the Doll House, the Circus Building, the Weapons Exhibit, the Oriental Room, the Crown Jewel Collection, the Heritage of the Sea Building, and more.

75

Milwaukee County Trails

Oak Leaf Trail

Location & Setting
This trail began in 1939 as a 64 mile scenic loop around Milwaukee County by a dedicated group of bicycling enthusiasts. Today Oak Leaf Trail is recognized as one of the premier trail systems in the country. About 99 miles in length, the Oak Leaf Trail is composed of 42 miles of off-road asphalt paved path, 31 miles of parkway drives, and 26 miles of municipal streets as connecting routes.

Information
Milwaukee County Parks   414/257-6100
Milwaukee County Visitors Bureau   414/273-3950

Hank Aaron State Trail
(a planned trail) See Milwaukee County Trails

Length
Over 10 miles (planned)

Surface
Asphalt

Location & Setting
The Hank Aaron State Trail is a planned trail running from the Lakeshore State Park westerly through the city of Milwaukee to Doyne Park. There is a completed segment near Miller Park Stadium, and a temporary trail between 13th and 21st streets and 16th and 26th streets. These sections are asphalt paved. This trail will be the key east-west connection for cyclists, paralleling the I-94 corridor along the Menominee River down in the valley.

Getting There
There will be several access points designated as the trail is developed.

Information
Wisconsin Dept of Natural Resources   414/263-8559

www.dnr.state.wi.us/org/land/parks

Milwaukee derives its name from "Millocki" which mean "Gathering Place by the Waters". It was here that Native American Indians met for their summer encampments.

Milwaukee is made up of many ethnic neighborhoods, suburban communities, and historic districts. There are numerous festivals and ethnic celebrations from late spring through the fall.

Milwaukee County trails and bikeways are posted with directions signs.

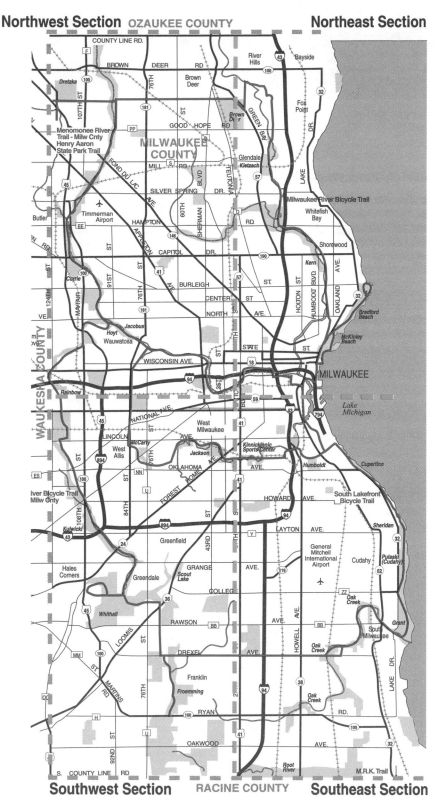

Milwaukee County Trails (continued)

Northwest Section

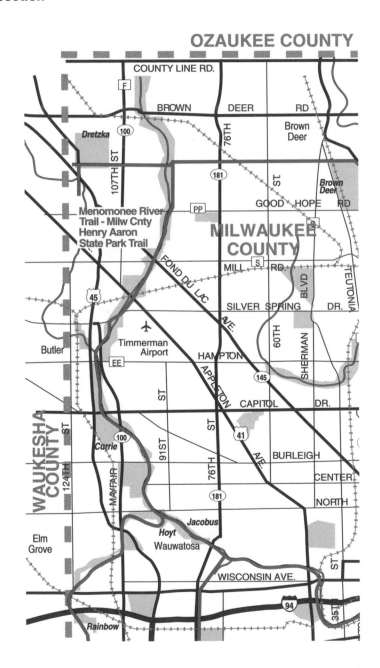

Northeast Section

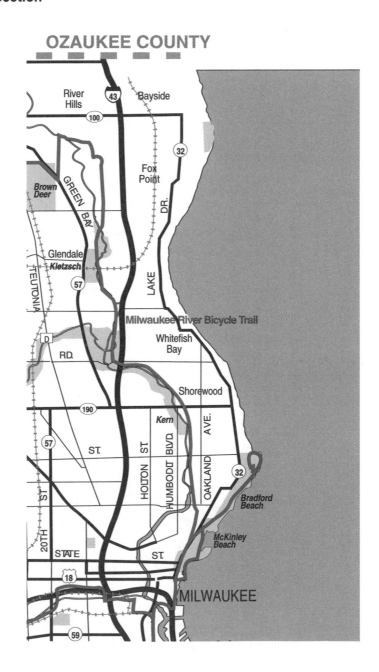

Southwest Section

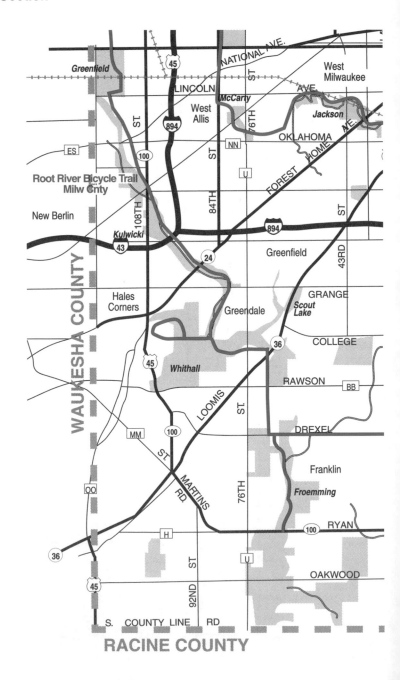

Southeast Section

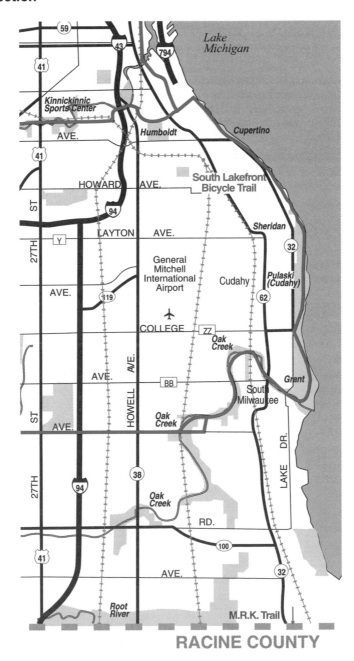

Milwaukee County Trails (continued)

Facilities in Route at adjoining Milwaukee County Parks
(Those adjoining the Leaf and Henry Aaron State Trail)

Bradford Beach 2400 N. Lincoln
Beach, Concessions

Brown Deer 7815 N. Green Bay Road
Picnic Area
Restrooms

Cupertino 2000 E. Iron Street
Restrooms

Currie 3535 N. Mayfair Road
Concession
Restrooms

Dretzka 12020 W. Bradley Road
Picnic area
Restrooms

Froemming 8801 S. 51 St.
Picnic Area
Restrooms

Grant 110 E. Hawthorne Avenue
Beach, Concessions
Lodging
Picnic Area
Restrooms

Greenfield 2028 S. 124 St.
Concessions
Aquatic Park
Picnic Area
Restrooms

Hoyt 1800 Swan Blvd.
Restrooms
Picnic Area

Humboldt 3000 S. Howell Avenue
Picnic Area
Restrooms

Jackson 3500 W. Forest Home Avenue
Picnic Area
Restrooms

Jacobus 6501 W. Hillside Lane
Picnic Area
Restrooms

Kern 3614 N. Humboldt Blvd
Picnic Area
Restrooms

Kinnickinnic Sports Center 3070 S. 20th
Street
Restrooms

Kletzsch 6560 N. Milwaukee River Parkway
Picnic Area
Restrooms

Kulwicki 10777 W. Coldspring Road
Picnic Area
Restrooms

McCarty 8214 W. Cleveland Avenue
Picnic Area
Restrooms

McKinley 1750 N. Lincoln Memorial Drive
Beach
Concessions

Oak Creek Parkway
Picnic Area
Restrooms

Pulaski-Cudahy 5400 S. Swift Avenue
Picnic Area
Restrooms

Rainbow 700 S. 119th Street
Picnic Area
Restrooms

Root River Parkway
Picnic Area
Restrooms

Scout Lake 5902 W. Loomis Road
Picnic Area
Restrooms

Sheridan 3800 S. Lake Drive
Concessions
Picnic Area
Restrooms

Whitnall 5829 S. 92nd Street
Botanical Gardens
Concessions
Nature Center
Overnight Lodge
Picnic Area
Restrooms

The Bicycle Federation of Wisconsin

(continued from page 69)

The Bicycle Federation of Wisconsin and Livable Communities

Tne way to have your voice heard is to join an organization which firmly supports communitycontrol of ISTEA funds. In Wisconsin, the major proponent of ISTEA is the Bicycle Federation of Wisconsin (the League of American Bicyclists and Rails-to-Trails Conservancy have been quite effective on the national level).

The Bicycle Federation of Wisconsin, a statewide non-profit, membership-based organization, firmly believes that the more people on bikes, the more livable the community. The notion of bikeability and livability is what propels the BFW into the thick of the struggle to maintain community control over ISTEA funds. Over the past five years communities have made the clear choice to rebuild their human-scaled infrastructure through ISTEA; the BFW wants this to continue.

Safe Roads for All

The Bicycle Federation of Wisconsin is also heavily involved in bicycle safety issues, such as education of motorists about cyclists' rights to the road, and effective cycling techniques for cyclists of all ages. The Bicycle Federation of Wisconsin won a major legislative victory in 19961 with the passage of the Bicycle Safety Bill (AB 96), which provided for uniform and updated statutes regarding bicyclists statewide. The bicycle is now clearly and definitively a legal vehicle with all of the rights and responsibilities of any other road user.

Currently the Bicycle Federation of Wisconsin is a member of the State Bicycle Advisory Committee. The Bicycle Federation of Wisconsin is pressing for the State Bike Plan to forthrightly state that bicyclists will be seriously considered in all state-sponsored road projects.

Members Are Our Strength

The Bicycle Federation is membership driven. Please join us in the push for community friendly transportation. Bicycle Federation of Wisconsin is a membership organization which promotes bikeable communities. Annual memberships are $25 (a personal benefit is a 10 % discount at 35 bike shops and bike-friendly businesses statewide). Inquiries can be addressed to:

Bicycle Federation of Wisconsin
www.bfw.org

Mountain Bay Trail

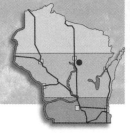

Length	83 miles
Surface	Compacted limestone (asphalt paved in Shawano)
Location & Setting	This trail is built on the former Chicago & Northwestern railroad right-of way in east central Wisconsin. Named for the two geological features, it connects, Rib Mountain in Marathon County and Green Bay in Brown County. The Mountain-Bay Trail passes farms, woods, wetlands, small town and a spruce bog. The kettles, eskers, and moraines of glacial terrain are visible. There is a prairie remnant on the west side of the trail just south of Cty B, south of Pulaski.
Getting There	There are numerous access points from the communities and road connections along this trail.

East Trailhead: Memorial Park in Howard, on Cty HS, a half mile northwest of the Hwy 141/Velp Avenue exit.

West Trailhead: From hwy 29, north on Cty X to Schofield Avenue, then east one mile to Weston Municipal Center. Continue north one block on Municipal Street to a parking lot.

Information	Brown County Parks	920/448-4466
	Shawano County Parks	715/524-5166
	Marathon County Parks	715/261-1550

www.shawano.com www.wausaucvb.com

County	Brown, Shawano, Marathon

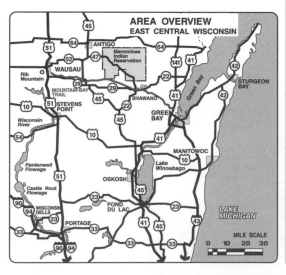

Mountain-Bay Trail Route Slip

	SECT	FROM	TO
Howard			83.0
To Pulaski	12.0	12.0	71.0
Zachow	8.0	20.0	63.0
Banduel	5.0	25.0	58.0
Shawano	9.0	34.0	49.0
Gresham	10.0	44.0	39.0
Bowler	10.0	54.0	29.0
Shepley	6.0	60.0	23.0
Eland	2.0	68.0	15.0
Hatley	4.0	72.0	11.0
Ringle	5.0	77.0	6.0
Weston	6.0	83.0	

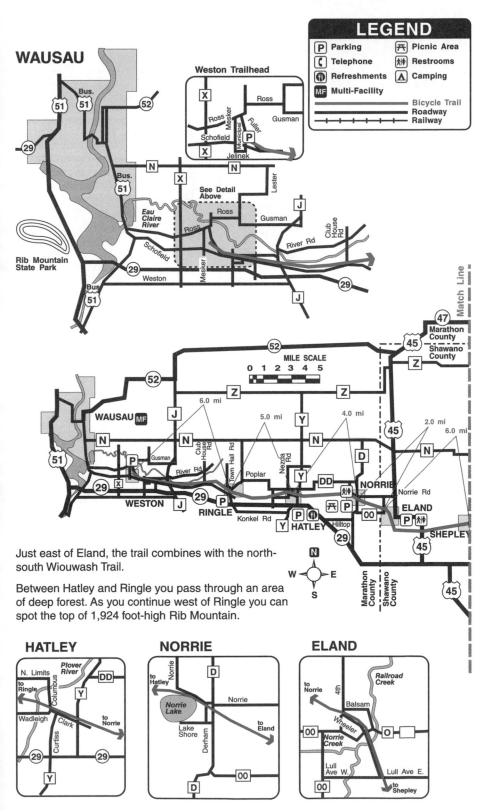

LEGEND

P	Parking	🍴	Picnic Area
C	Telephone	🚻	Restrooms
🥤	Refreshments	A	Camping
MF	Multi-Facility		

━━━━━ Bicycle Trail
━━━━━ Roadway
┼┼┼┼┼ Railway

WAUSAU

Weston Trailhead

Ross
Mesker
Fuller
Gusman
Schofield
Municipal
Jelinek

See Detail Above

Eau Claire River
Ross
Gusman
Club House Rd
River Rd
Schofield
Rib Mountain State Park
Weston
Mesker

Match Line

Marathon County
Shawano County

MILE SCALE
0 1 2 3 4 5

WAUSAU MF
6.0 mi
5.0 mi
4.0 mi
2.0 mi
6.0 mi

Gusman
Club House Rd
Town Hall Rd
Nezda Rd
River Rd
Poplar
NORRIE
Norrie Rd
WESTON
RINGLE
Konkel Rd
HATLEY
Hilltop
ELAND
SHEPLEY

Just east of Eland, the trail combines with the north-south Wiouwash Trail.

Between Hatley and Ringle you pass through an area of deep forest. As you continue west of Ringle you can spot the top of 1,924 foot-high Rib Mountain.

Marathon County | Shawano County

HATLEY

N. Limits
Plover River
DD
to Ringle
Columbus
Y
Wadleigh
Clark
to Norrie
Curtiss
29
29
Y

NORRIE

Norrie
to Hatley
D
Norrie
Norrie Lake
to Eland
Lake Shore
Derham
00
D

ELAND

Railroad Creek
to Norrie
4th
Balsam
Wheeler
00
Norrie Creek
O
Lull Ave W.
Lull Ave E.
00
to Shepley

85

Mountain Bay Trail (continued)

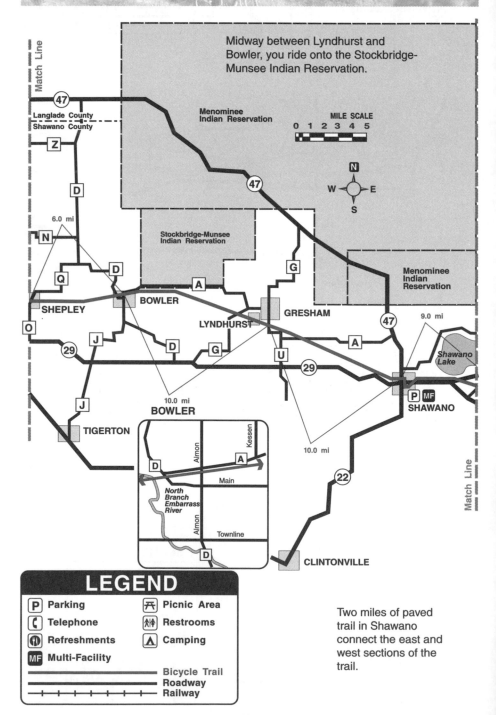

Midway between Lyndhurst and Bowler, you ride onto the Stockbridge-Munsee Indian Reservation.

Match Line

47

Langlade County
Shawano County

Z

Menominee
Indian Reservation

MILE SCALE
0 1 2 3 4 5

D

6.0 mi

N

Q

D

47

Stockbridge-Munsee
Indian Reservation

N
W   E
S

SHEPLEY

BOWLER

A

G

Menominee
Indian
Reservation

O

J

29

D

LYNDHURST

GRESHAM

47

9.0 mi

G

A

Shawano
Lake

U

29

P MF

SHAWANO

J

10.0 mi
BOWLER

TIGERTON

Kessen

Almon

D

A

Main

10.0 mi

North
Branch
Embarrass
River

Almon

Townline

22

D

CLINTONVILLE

Match Line

LEGEND

P	Parking	🎪	Picnic Area
📞	Telephone	🚻	Restrooms
🍴	Refreshments	⛺	Camping
MF	Multi-Facility		

——————— Bicycle Trail
——————— Roadway
+++++++ Railway

Two miles of paved trail in Shawano connect the east and west sections of the trail.

Trail passes are required on the Mountain-Bay Trail. Daily passes are available at self-registration managed trails, or the Wisconsin Dept. of Natural Resources, and are valid at all state trails.

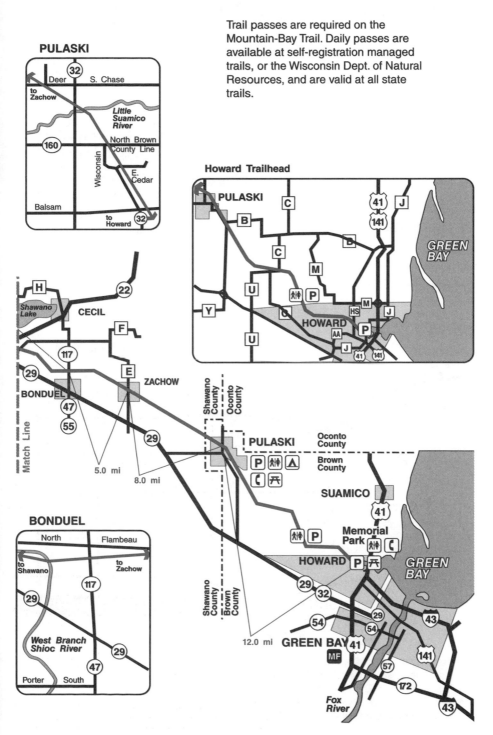

PULASKI

Deer   S. Chase

to Zachow

Little Suamico River

160

North Brown County Line

Wisconsin

E. Cedar

Balsam

to Howard   32

Howard Trailhead

PULASKI   C   41   J

B   141

C   D

M

U

Y   P

U   HS   M   J

HOWARD   P

AA

J   41   141

H   22

Shawano Lake   CECIL

F

117

29   E   ZACHOW

BONDUEL

47

55

Match Line

5.0 mi   29   8.0 mi

Shawano County / Oconto County

PULASKI   Oconto County

P   A   Brown County

C

SUAMICO   41

BONDUEL

North   Flambeau

to Shawano   to Zachow

117

29

West Branch Shioc River   29

Porter   South

47

P   Memorial Park   C

HOWARD   P   GREEN BAY

Shawano County / Brown County

29   32

12.0 mi   GREEN BAY   41

MF

54   29   43

54

141

57

172

Fox River   43

GREEN BAY

87

New Berlin Recreational Trail

Length	6.5 miles
Surface	Paved (2005)
Location & Setting	This east-west 6.5 mile, 10 foot wide trail runs along a power line next to a railroad right-of way. It's relatively flat and the surface is paved. The east trailhead is at Greenfield Park, where it connects with the Oak Leaf Trail. Facilities include parking, water, and restrooms. From the western end of the trail in Waukesha, you can take city streets for 1.5 miles to connect with the Fox River Trail or the glacial DrumlinTrail.
Getting There	East trailhead: Greenfield Park, at 124th Street, south of Greenfield Avenue.
	West Trailhead: Springdale Road, south of Rte 59 in Waukesha.
Information	Waukesha County Parks 262/548-7790
	www.midwestroads.com
County	Waukesha

Minooka Park Hiking Trail
Length: 6.0 miles
Surface: Natural-groomed, wood chips
Setting: Wooded, hilly, open fields

Minooka Park, part of the Waukesha County Park system, is located south of the New Berlin Trail on Racine Avenue (Cty Y). Additional facilities and activities include parking, restrooms, drinking water, picnicking, swimming and sledding.

Oconto River State Trail

Length	30 miles
Surface	Limestone screenings, ballast, graded stone
Location & Setting	A 30 mile former railroad railbed, running between Gillett and Townsend, in northeastern Wisconsin. It parallels the Oconto River, a popular destination for float trips and fishing. About 5 miles of trail around Lakewood is surfaced with limestone screenings. The remainder varies from ballast to natural graded material. The trail crosses many creeks and branches of the Oconto River as it proceeds north into the Nicolet National Forest.
Getting There	Gillett is located 14 miles west of Hwy 141 and 22/32, and is about 42 miles northwest of Green Bay.
Information	Oconto County Forestry & Parks 920/834-6995 National Park Service Office 608/264-5610
County	Oconto

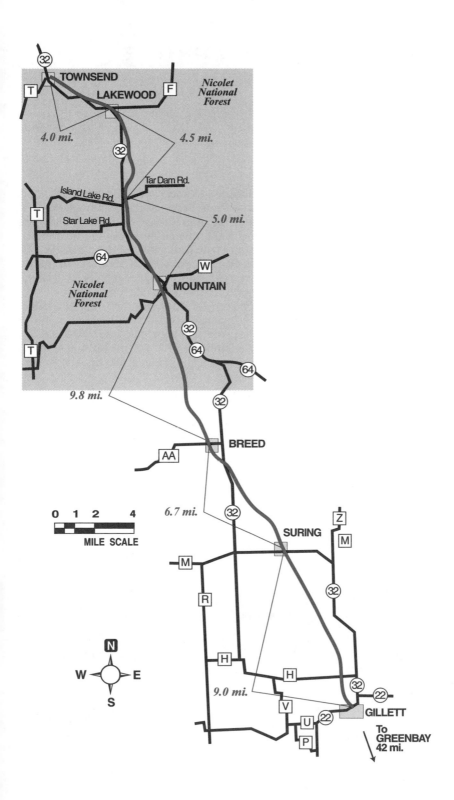

TOWNSEND

LAKEWOOD

Nicolet
National
Forest

T

F

4.0 mi.

4.5 mi.

Tar Dam Rd.

Island Lake Rd.

Star Lake Rd.

T

5.0 mi.

W

Nicolet
National
Forest

MOUNTAIN

T

9.8 mi.

BREED

AA

0 1 2   4
MILE SCALE

6.7 mi.

SURING

Z

M

M

R

32

N
W   E
S

H

H

9.0 mi.

V

32

22

U

22

GILLETT

P

To
GREENBAY
42 mi.

91

Old Abe State Trail

Length	17 miles
Surface	Asphalt
Location & Setting	A 17 mile linear trail between Cornell and The Chippewa River, just west of lake Wissota State Park in northwest Wisconsin. The surface is asphalt, and the setting is forest and open area. At Cornell, there is a 1.2 mile city trail linking to Brunet Island State Park. Currently, the trail ends at the Chippewa River, just west of Lake Wissota State Park. Six miles of trail connecting the southern trailhead to Chippewa Falls have been constructed or are planned, and will include a new bridge across the Chippewa River. "Old Abe" was the name of a bald eagle mascot of the 8th Wisconsin Regiment formed near Jim Falls during the civil War. You'll enjoy some gorgeous views as the trail parallels the Chippewa River to Jim Falls. A short distance off the trail on Cty S in Jim Falls is an Old Abe statue and memorial.
Getting There	Chippewa Falls is located at the intersection of Hwy 84, 53, and 12 in West Central Wisconsin. From Chippewa Falls, north on Hwy 178, which parallels the west side of the Chippewa River, to get to the town of Cornell and the northern trailhead.
Information	Chippewa Area Visitors Center 715/723-0331 Chippewa County Forest & Parks 715/726-7880 **www.chippewachamber.org**
County	Chippewa

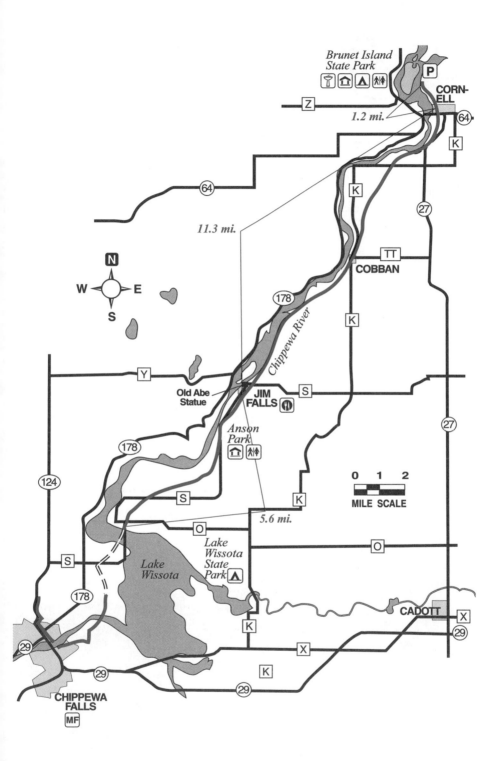

Brunet Island
State Park

CORN-
ELL

Z

1.2 mi.

64

K

64

K

27

11.3 mi.

TT

COBBAN

N

W E

S

178

Chippewa River

K

Y

Old Abe
Statue

JIM
FALLS

S

Anson
Park

178

124

S

0 1 2

MILE SCALE

K

O

5.6 mi.

Lake
Wissota
State
Park

O

S

Lake
Wissota

178

CADOTT

X

29

K

29

X

X

K

CHIPPEWA
FALLS

MF

29

29

93

Old Plank Road Trail

Length & Surface Asphalt – 8 foot wide with a parallel 8 foot turf surface for horses

Location & Setting The Old Plank Road Trail is a 17 mile multi-purpose trail connecting the Lake Michigan Lakefront of Sheboygan to historic Greenbush and the Ice Age National Trail. It parallels Hwy 23, the original wooden plank road route of the mid-1800's. It's asphalt paved and the grade is moderate, with trail markers, parks, picnic areas, and emergency telephones. Road crossings are frequent. In the village of Greenbush, you can tour the Wade House, a restored stagecoach inn from the plank road days. There are interconnecting trails that lead you to many of the area's popular attractions like the Kohler Village, Sheboygan Falls and its historic Main Street, and historic Plymouth.

Getting There The east trailhead is at the intersection of Hwy 43 and 23. Exit Hwy 43 onto 23, and proceed east one mile to Taylor Avenue. Turn right to Erie Street, then right again to the end of the road, which is the trailhead. The trail passes under Hwy 43.

Information Sheboygan County Planning Resources Dept.   920/459-3060
Sheboygan Visitors Bureau   920/457-9495

ohwy.com/wi/o/olplrdtr.htm

County Sheboygan

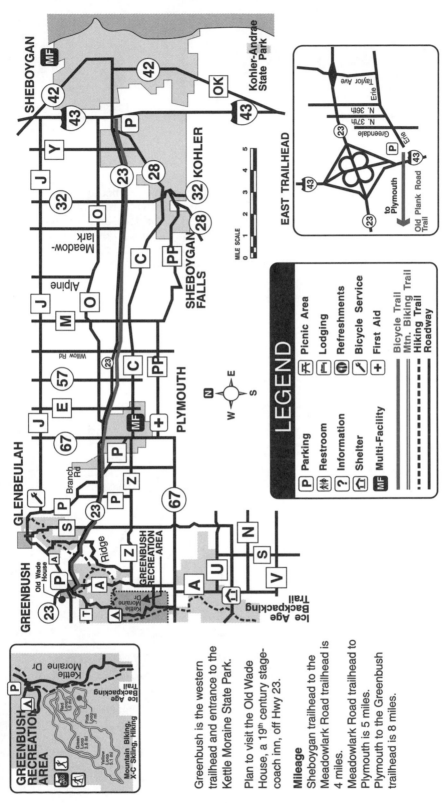

LEGEND

P Parking	✚ Picnic Area		
RR Restroom	🏠 Lodging		
? Information	🍴 Refreshments		
⤺ Shelter	🔧 Bicycle Service		
MF Multi-Facility	✚ First Aid		

— — — Bicycle Trail
· · · · · Mtn. Biking Trail
– – – – Hiking Trail
———— Roadway

EAST TRAILHEAD

GREENBUSH RECREATION AREA

Mountain Biking, X-C Skiing, Hiking

Red Loop 1.5 mi
Pink Loop .7 mi
Green Loop 3.6 mi
Yellow Loop 5.1 mi

Kettle Moraine Dr

Ice Age Backpacking Trail

Greenbush is the western trailhead and entrance to the Kettle Moraine State Park.

Plan to visit the Old Wade House, a 19th century stage-coach inn, off Hwy 23.

Mileage

Sheboygan trailhead to the Meadowlark Road trailhead is 4 miles.

Meadowlark Road trailhead to Plymouth is 5 miles.

Plymouth to the Greenbush trailhead is 8 miles.

Omaha Trail

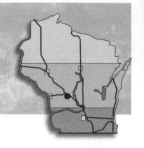

Length	13 miles one way
Surface	Limestone screenings
Location & Setting	The Omaha Trail is built on former railroad bed between Elroy and Camp Douglas. The setting is farmland, rock bluffs, and wooded areas. The route includes 17 bridges, an overpass, and some steep walled valleys as it climbs to an 850 foot long tunnel south of Hustler near the southern end of the trail. The trail connects to the Elroy-Sparta Trail in Elroy.
Getting There	Camp Douglas is located less than a mile south of Hwy 90/94. Elroy is located at the junction of Hwy 8 and & 71.
Information	Elroy Commons Bike Trails & Tourist 608/462-2453 Juneau County Forestry & Parks 608/847-9389

www.altrails.com/rail/wi.omaha.html

County Juneau

County passes are required to use the trail for all individual 16 years old or older. Passes can be purchased in Elroy, Hustler, and in Camp Douglas.

Camp Douglas is a village with both Army and Air National Guard installations nearby. Guided bus tours are available.

Mill Bluff State Park

CAMP DOUGLAS

Little Lemonweir River

2.5 mi

HUSTLER

Olson Rd

TUNNEL

NEW LISBON

2.5 mi

to Sparta

The Omaha Trail

KENDALL

Elroy-Sparta Trail

4.3 mi

MAUSTON

MILE SCALE
0 1 2 3

3.2 mi

ELROY

UNION CENTER

"400" Trail

to Reedsburg

LEGEND

🎋	Picnic Area	P	Parking
?	Information	🚻	Restrooms
🍴	Refreshments	🛏	Lodging
MF	Multi-Facility		

Bicycle Trail
Roadway

Osaugie Trail

Length & Surface	5 miles Asphalt paved
Location & Setting	The Osaugie Trail is located in the city of Superior and is part of the Tri-County Recreation Corridor Trail. It parallels Hwy 2/53 and the city's harbor, which is the busiest on the Great Lakes. It passes under the immense Burlington Ore Dock. Nearby attractions include harbor views, Wisconsin Point, the S.S. Meteor Museum, Amnicon State Park, and Pattison State Park where Big Manitou Fall, Wisconsin's highest waterfall at 165 feet, plunges into a deep gorge of the Black River. The 4.6 mile on-road side trip takes you to Wisconsin Point, a slender sand bar with miles of beaches guarding the entrance to the harbor.
Getting There	The trailhead is located at Harbor View Park in Superior at the intersection of Belknap Street (Hwy 2) and Harbor View Parkway (Hwy 2/53).
Information	Superior-Douglas County Visitors Bureau 800/942-5313 Superior Parks & Recreation 715/394-0270 **www.visitsuperior.com**
County	Douglas

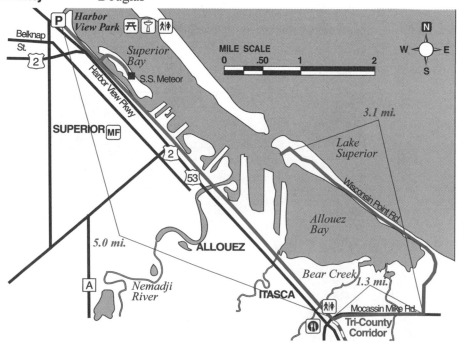

97

Ozaukee Interurban Trail

Length	30 miles
Surface	Mostly paved with about 4 miles of roads
Location & Setting	The Ozaukee Interurban Trail is a 30 mile paved trail spanning the length of Ozaukee County. Most of the trail is off-road and perfect for family enjoyment. It connects the communities of Mequon, Thiensville, Cedarburg, Grafton, Port Washington and Belgium by using the right-of way owned by the We Energies (the electricity service company). The trail connects historic downtowns with natural landscapes, including hardwood woodlands, wetlands, Cedar Creek, the Milwaukee River, and Lake Michigan. Trail use is free, and is intended for year round uses. Motorized vehicles and horses are not allowed.
Getting There	The south trailhead is located on County Line Road, a few blocks west of Cedarburg Road.
	The north trailhead is located at the Sheboygan County Line west of Hwy 43.
	Parking is available at the municipal lot on Buntrock Avenue west of Main Street in Thiensville near the south trailhead and at the Village Park at 106 Beach Street in Belgium near the north trailhead.
Information	Ozaukee County Tourism Council 877/875-7795
	www.ozaukeetourism.com
County	Ozaukee

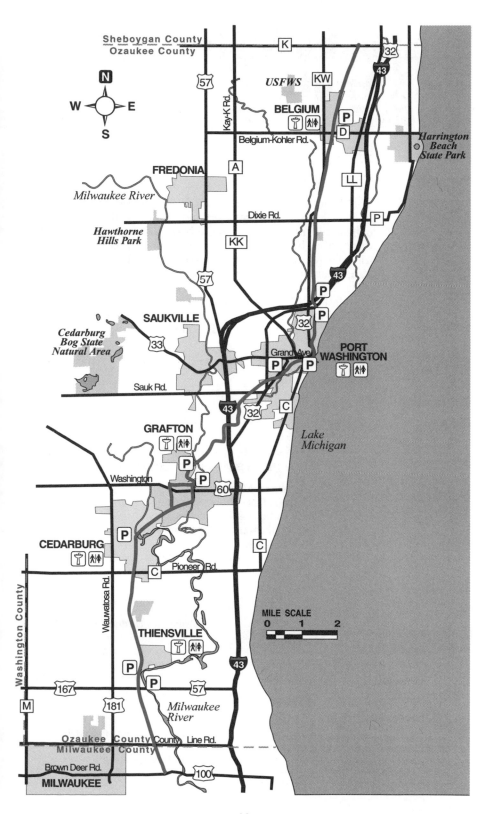

Sheboygan County
Ozaukee County

N
W E
S

K

57

USFWS   KW

BELGIUM

P

D

Kay-K Rd.

Belgium-Kohler Rd.

32

43

Harrington
Beach
State Park

FREDONIA

A

Milwaukee River

Dixie Rd.

LL

P

Hawthorne
Hills Park

KK

57

43

Cedarburg
Bog State
Natural Area

SAUKVILLE

33

P

P

32

PORT
WASHINGTON

Sauk Rd.

Grand Ave.

P

P

43

32

C

GRAFTON

Lake
Michigan

P

Washington

P

60

CEDARBURG

P

C

Wauwatosa Rd.

Pioneer Rd.

C

MILE SCALE
0   1   2

Washington County

THIENSVILLE

P

P

43

167

181

57

M

Milwaukee
River

Ozaukee County   County Line Rd.
Milwaukee County

Brown Deer Rd.

100

MILWAUKEE

Pecatonica State Park Trail

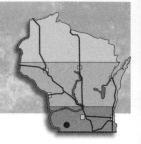

Length	10 miles
Surface	Crushed stone
Location & Setting	This 10 mile one way trail goes through the Bonner Branch river valley past pastures, wetlands, and woodlands, and was converted from former railroad bed. In season you can find raspberries, blackberries and wild grapes to pick along the trail. There are 24 bridges to cross. The valley becomes deeper, steeper, and more wooded in the eastern part, and widens into a marshy area west of Calamine. At Calamine, the Pecatonica Trail links with the Cheese Country Trail. About three miles north of the Belmont trailhead is Belmont Mound State Park, which offers scenic views of an area including parts of three states.
Getting There	From Darlington, take Hwy 23 north to Hwy 23, then west 3.5 miles to Calamine.
Information	Pacatonica State Park Trail 608/523-4427
County	Lafayette

The present trail ends about a ½ mile west of Main Street (Hwy 151) in Belmont and 300 feet south of Hwy G.

Platteville Attractions:
Chicago Bear Summer Training Camp
UW-Platteville – Southwest Road
Mining Museum & Rollo Jamison Museum
405 East Main Street
Wisconsin Shakespeare Festival
UW-Platteville Center for the Arts

LEGEND

🏕	Picnic Area	🅿	Parking
❓	Information	🚻	Restrooms
🍴	Refreshments	🛏	Lodging
MF	Multi-Facility		

━━━━━━━━ Bicycle Trail
= = = = = = = = Proposed Trail
▪▪▪▪▪▪▪▪▪▪▪▪▪ Alternate Trail
━━━━━━━━ Roadway

Governor Dodge State Park
Located 3 miles north of Dodgeville on State Hwy 23. It is the 2nd largest state park in Wisconsin. The terrain in the park is rugged and varies from steep hills and sandstone bluffs to deep lush valleys. Activities include hiking, horseback riding, swimming, picnicking, and camping. There is a park admission fee.

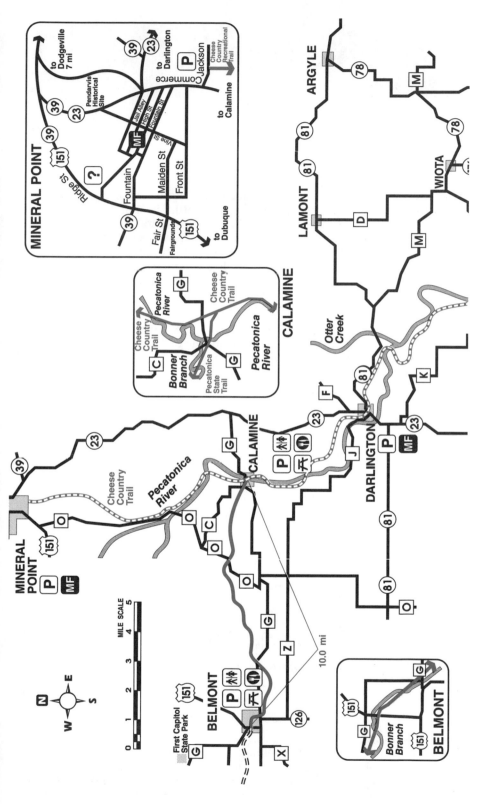

MINERAL POINT

to Dodgeville 7 mi

to Darlington

23
39

Pendarvis Historical Site

Bell Alley
High St
Fountain St
Vine St

MF

?

Ridge St

151
39

23
39

39

Commerce

Jackson

P

Cheese Country Recreational Trail

to Calamine

to Dubuque

Fountain

Fair St

Maiden St

Front St

Fairgrounds

151

CALAMINE

Pecatonica River

Cheese Country Trail

Cheese Country Trail

Pecatonica River

Bonner Branch

Pecatonica State Trail

G
C
G

BELMONT

Bonner Branch

151
G
G
151

ARGYLE

78

M

81

78

81

LAMONT

D

M

WIOTA

Otter Creek

81

K

F

23

81

DARLINGTON

P
MF
23

J

CALAMINE

G

P
禾
休
🚻

23

MINERAL POINT

P
MF

39

151

O

Cheese Country Trail

Pecatonica River

O

C

O

O

G

Z

126

10.0 mi

BELMONT

First Capitol State Park

151

P
禾
休
🚻

G

X

O

N
W E S

MILE SCALE
0 1 2 3 4 5

101

Pine Line Trail

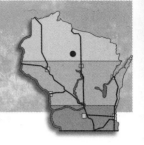

Length	26 miles
Surface	Crushed stone
Location & Setting	The Pine Line Trail is located in north central Wisconsin, with its south trailhead in Medford. The trail is marked, and follows the abandoned Wisconsin Central Railroad right-of way. The Pine Line passes through wooded glacial hills past numerous beaver ponds. The north portion of the trail runs through the 12,000 year old terminal moraine created by the Wisconsin Glacier. This area contains cedar swamps, bogs, and hills covered with hardwood forests, including wetlands with interesting vegetation.
Getting There	South trailhead: From Hwy 13 in Medford, proceed west on Allman Avenue on the north side of Medford for one mile to the parking area and a trail sign.
	North trailhead: trail ends at Morner Road, ½ mile east of Hwy 13 and 2 miles south of Prentice.
Information	Ice Age Park & Trail Foundation 715/748-2030
	Price County Tourism 800/269-4505
	Taylor County Tourism 888/682-9567
	www.altrails.com/rai/wi/pineline.html
County	Price Taylor

AREA OVERVIEW

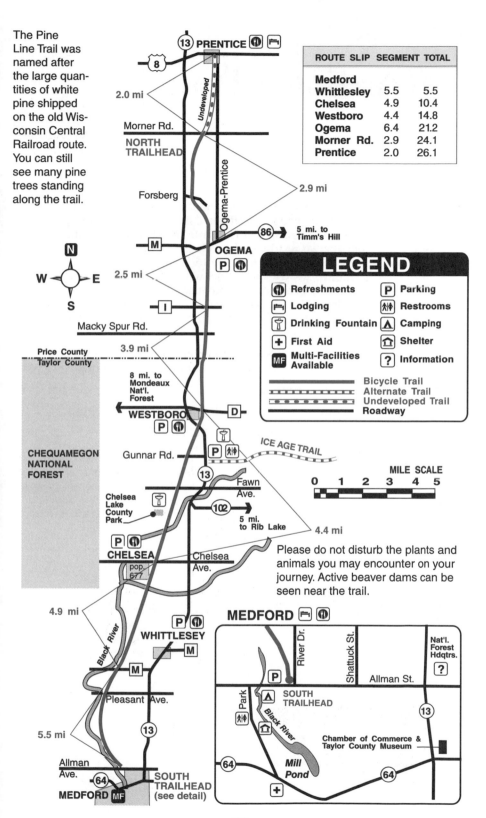

The Pine Line Trail was named after the large quantities of white pine shipped on the old Wisconsin Central Railroad route. You can still see many pine trees standing along the trail.

ROUTE SLIP	SEGMENT	TOTAL
Medford		
Whittlesley	5.5	5.5
Chelsea	4.9	10.4
Westboro	4.4	14.8
Ogema	6.4	21.2
Morner Rd.	2.9	24.1
Prentice	2.0	26.1

LEGEND

- Refreshments
- Lodging
- Drinking Fountain
- First Aid
- Multi-Facilities Available (MF)
- Parking
- Restrooms
- Camping
- Shelter
- Information

Bicycle Trail
Alternate Trail
Undeveloped Trail
Roadway

MILE SCALE
0 1 2 3 4 5

Please do not disturb the plants and animals you may encounter on your journey. Active beaver dams can be seen near the trail.

103

Pine River Recreational Trail

Length	16 miles
Surface	Limestone screenings
Location & Setting	The trail connects the communities of Richland Center and Lone Rock, and was built on abandoned railroad bed paralleling the western side of Hwy 14. The area is rural with popular tourist areas nearby such as House on the Rock and governor Dodge State Park. There are 15 bridge crossings, and the trail traverses several distinct wildlife habitats. A designated bikeway is planned along Kennedy Road between Lone Rock and Spring Green, which would connect to the bikeway along Hwy 23 south to the House on the rock and near Governor Dodge State Park.
Getting There	The Trailhead in Richland Center is located on Bohman Drive, along Hwy 14, and near the Richland Square Shopping Center.
Information	Richland County Tourism Center 608/647-6148

backroadbike.com/pinetrail.html

County Richland, Sauk

There is a four foot designated bikeway on either side of Hwy 23 out of Spring Green. This continues south on to the House on the Rock and near Governor Dodge State Park.

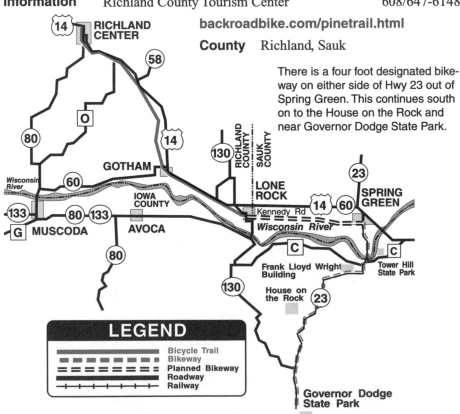

Racine County Trails

Length   Overall: 22 miles, plus over 100 miles of designated bikeways

Surface   Crushed limestone, asphalt along sections of the Seven Waters Trail

Location & Setting

Seven Waters Trail
This trail is an 11mile trail between Bushnell Park, south of Burlington and north to the Milwaukee County line. Surface is crushed limestone except for a section around Waterford.

North Shore
This 3 mile trail begins north of Hwy 11, travels south through Elmwood Park and across Cty KR into Kenosha County, connecting to the Pike Bike Trail.

Racine/Sturtevant Trail
This 3 mile trail provides a route westward from the North Shore Trail. It extends to Willow Road with a marked connection to Pritchard Park. There are plans to extend the trail to Cty H and eventually to I-94.

MRK Trail
This trail covers 5 miles and begins west of Michna Road at 7 Mile Road, south to 3 Mile Road and into the city of Racine. Numerous accesses are available along the several trails and the 100 miles of designated bike routes.

Lake Michigan Pathway
The Lake Michigan Pathway extends approximately 9.8 miles along the Racine Lakeshore connecting the 5 miles long MRK Trail on the north with the 3 mile long North Shore Trail on the south. Points of interest in route include the Dekoven Center, Pershing Park, Downtown Racine, the Harbor, North Beach and the Zoo. The Lake Michigan Pathway also connects at the Main Street Bridge to the Root River Pathway.

Root River Pathway
The Root River Pathway extends 4 miles from the Main Street Bridge on the east to Colonial Park on the west. It also connects to the MRK, North Shore and Racine/Sturtevant Trails. The Root River Pathway begins where the city began and takes one along the Root River, past the headquarters of the Case Company and the former Western Publishing headquarters before entering Colonial Park.

Information

Racine County Public Works	262/886-8440
Racine County Visitors Bureau	800/272-2463

www/racineco.com/public works/

Racine County Trails (continued)

Circling the county is a 100 mile marked bicycle trip. It is a combination of off-road trails and rural roadways. The sights along the route include the Michigan Wildlife Refuge, Root and Lower Fox Rivers, Racine Zoo, and the Frank Lloyd Wright designed corporate headquarters of Johnson Wax.

Colonel Heg Memorial Park contains a museum highlighting the unique heritage of early Norwegian settlers. It is the setting of Heritage Day, held in June each year. The park offers picnic areas and a comfort station.

Cliffside Park offers a winding nature trail through a wooded ravine, a children's play area, and reservable picnic areas with table and grills. The park has family campsites, comfort stations, and a sanitary station for RV campers.

Sanders Park features a marked nature trail through 30 acres. Over 90 species of native wildflowers are found here. The park has campsites, a comfort station and a sanitary station for RV campers.

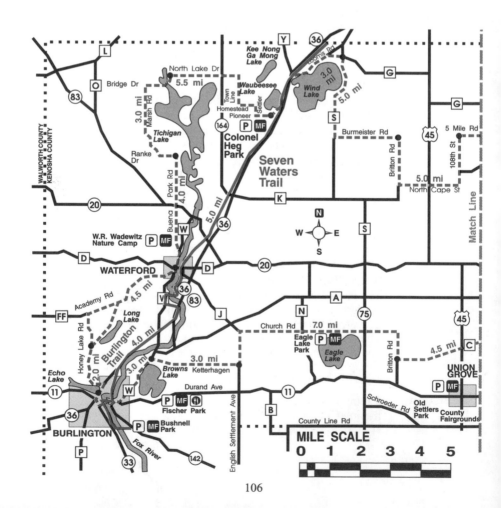

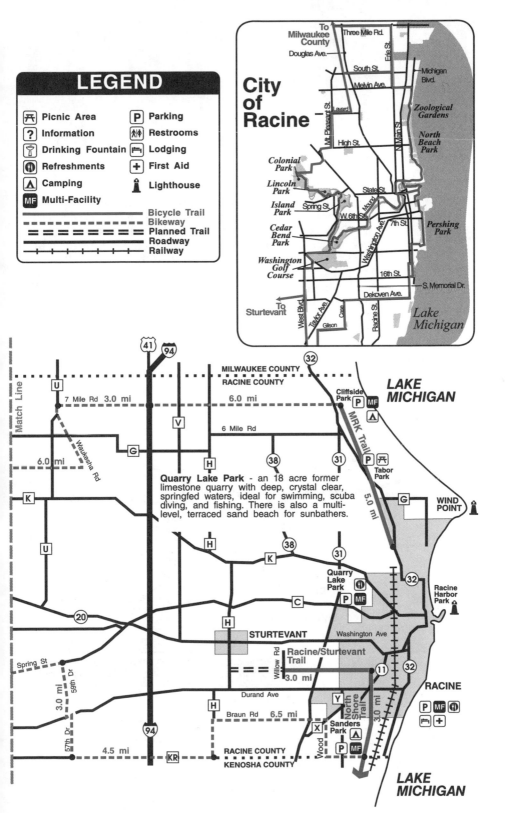

Red Cedar State Trail

Length	15 miles
Surface	Crushed limestone
Location & Setting	A 15 mile easy to ride, crushed limestone rail-trail between Menomonie and the Chippewa River crossing at the southern end. From Menomonee, the trail parallels the west bank of the river for nearly 8 miles through Irvington to the little town of Downsville. At Downsville, you'll cross the river to follow its east bank seven miles south to Dunnville. From Dunnville you'll continue another 1.5 mile through the Dunnville Wildlife Area before crossing the Chippewa River on an 800 foot stressed iron bridge to the junction with the Chippewa River State Trail. The setting includes beautiful bluffs and scenic views of the Red Cedar River.
Getting There	The Menomonie trailhead is at the Depot on 11th Avenue (Hwy 29) in Menomonie.
Information	Red Cedar State Trail 715/232-1242 Chippewa Valley Visitors Bureau 888/523-3866 **www.chippewavalley.net**
County	Dunn

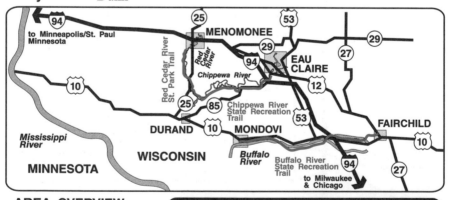

AREA OVERVIEW

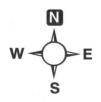

N
W — E
S

LEGEND

P	Parking	**👫**	Restrooms
🎋	Picnic Area	**🚰**	Drinking Fountain
🛏	Lodging	**🍴**	Refreshments
MF	Multi-Facility		

━━━━━━ Bicycle Trail
━━━━━━ Roadway

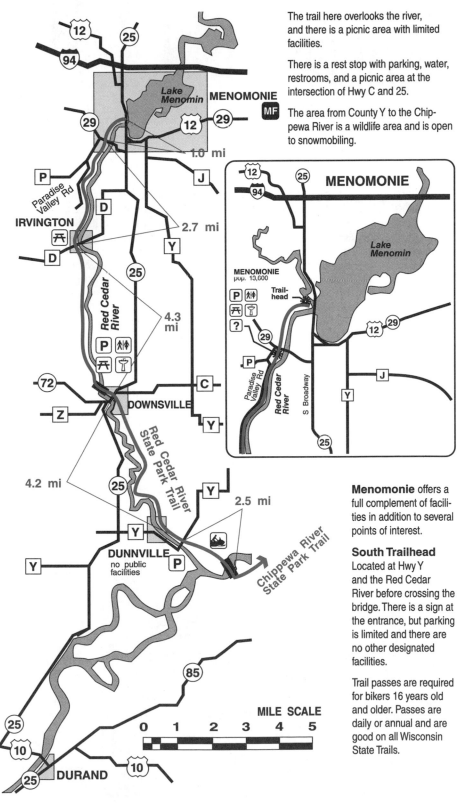

The trail here overlooks the river, and there is a picnic area with limited facilities.

There is a rest stop with parking, water, restrooms, and a picnic area at the intersection of Hwy C and 25.

The area from County Y to the Chippewa River is a wildlife area and is open to snowmobiling.

MENOMONIE
pop. 13,000

Menomonie offers a full complement of facilities in addition to several points of interest.

South Trailhead
Located at Hwy Y and the Red Cedar River before crossing the bridge. There is a sign at the entrance, but parking is limited and there are no other designated facilities.

Trail passes are required for bikers 16 years old and older. Passes are daily or annual and are good on all Wisconsin State Trails.

MILE SCALE
0 1 2 3 4 5

Sugar River Trail

Length	23.5 miles
Surface	Limestone screenings, asphalt
Location & Setting	The Sugar River Trail is located in the pastoral landscape of Green County, with its red barns, green pastures, and black-and-white Holsteins. The trail follows the Sugar River southeast from New Glarus, passing through gently rolling hills, quarries, and woodlands. It is asphalt-paved in New Glarus and along the spur trail to New Glarus Woods State Park, and crushed limestone to Brodhead. Nearing Albany, the trail crosses the Sugar River on a long curving trestle. Between Albany and Brodhead you'll pass through the Clarence covered Bridge. The trail ends at Brodhead, where you'll find the two local campgrounds offering canoe trips down the river.
Getting There	North trailhead: New Glarus, at the depot on Railroad Street off Hwy 39 (6th Ave).
	South trailhead: Brodhead Exchange Street & West 3rd Street, 2 blocks west of Hwy 11.
Information	Broadhead Chamber of Commerce 608/897-8411 New Glarus Tourist 800/527-6838
	www.swisstown.com
	Sugar River State Trail 608/527-2334
	www.wiparks.net
County	Green

Trail Admission Fees

Trail passes required for bikers 16 years and older. Passes are daily or annual, and are valid on all Wisconsin State Trails. They are available at the trail headquarters in New Glarus, at New Glarus Woods State Park and at outlets in communities along the trail.

NEW GLARUS

Approximate distances from major cities:

Madison to New Glarus - 22 miles

Milwaukee to New Glarus - 100 miles

Chicago to Brodhead - 130 miles

NEW GLARUS ATTRACTIONS

(A) Information Booth

(B) Chalet of the Golden Fleece

(C) Swiss Historical Village

(D) Historical Marker (Hwy 69)

(E) Floral Clock

(F) Sugar River State Trail Headquarters

New Glarus, known as the 'Little Switzerland', was founded in 1845 by Swiss immigrants from Glarus, Switzerland. The trail headquarters, located here in a former Milwaukee Road depot, offers nature and history displays and a driver-only shuttle service.

New Glarus Events

Late June	Heidi Drama; Heidi Craft & Food Fair
	Little Switzerland Festival
Early August	Volksfest (Swiss Independence Day)
	Wilhelm Tell Drama in English & German

There are parking and picnic facilities in all the communities along the trail. Both New Glarus and Brodhead have public swimming pools. The local communities hold numerous festivals throughout the summer, including:

Albany Yesteryear Day & Country/Bluegrass Music Festival

Monticello Summerfest

History
The first inhabitants were Sauk and Fox Indians, followed by the Winnebagos. The Winnebagos were forced out of the area after the Black Hawk War in 1832. Settlers began arriving in 1845. The railroad began operation in 1872.

Geology
The land of the Sugar River Valley was formed in layers over millions of years as it was covered three times by seas and then by a glacier. The valley was flooded by melting glaciers, which dropped more than 200 feet of sand and gravel here and eroded the valley walls. On top of this is a deep layer of loamy soil, mostly level to gently sloping.

Sugar River Trail (continued)

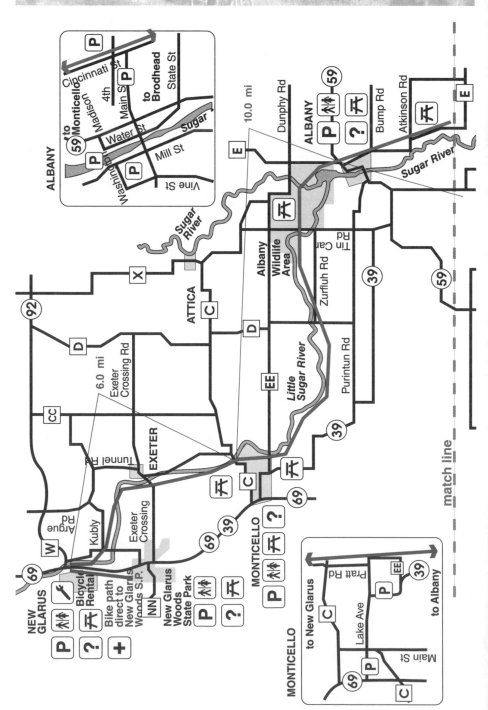

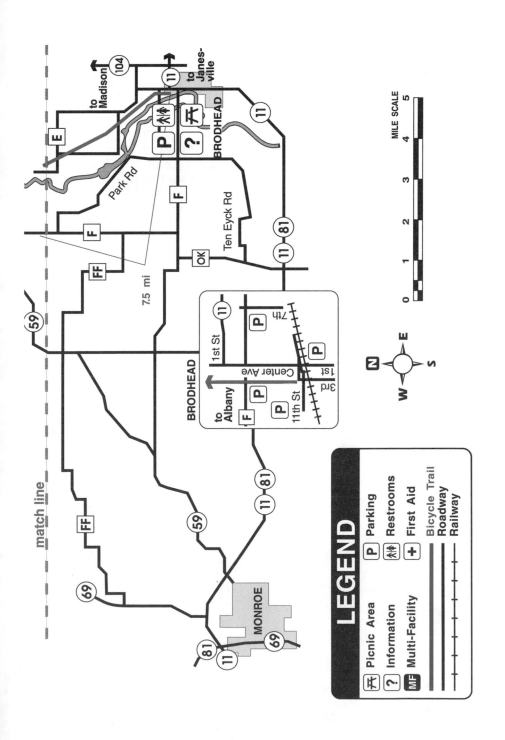

LEGEND

🏕 Picnic Area 🅿 Parking
❓ Information 🚻 Restrooms
MF Multi-Facility ➕ First Aid

———— Bicycle Trail
———— Roadway
—+—+— Railway

MILE SCALE

0 1 2 3 4 5

N

W — E

S

match line

to Madison

104

E

11

to Janes-ville

11

BRODHEAD

🅿 🚻 🏕 ❓

Park Rd

F

F

FF

7.5 mi

OK

Ten Eyck Rd

11 81

59

BRODHEAD

to Albany

1st St

11

🅿 7th

🅿

Center Ave

F 🅿

🅿 11th St

1st

3rd

FF

59

11 81

MONROE

81

11

69

69

113

Tomorrow River State Trail

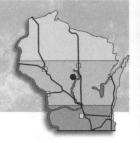

Length	14 miles
Surface	Crushed limestone
Location & Setting	This 14 mile trail was developed along an abandoned railroad grade. It is located in Central Wisconsin starting in the Village of Plover and ending at the Waupaca County line. The surface is crushed limestone, and is open to bicyclist, hikers, horseback riders, snowmobilers, skiers and dog sledders. The horse trail is a separate 9 mile parallel trail from Plover to Amherst Junction. It connects with the Green Circle Trail at Hoover Avenue, just north of Plover Road. Trail passes are required. Future plans are to extend the trail another 14 miles through Waupaca County.
Getting There	There is parking at Lake Emily Park on the east site of the lake on Lake Road in Amherst Junction, and at Cate Park.
Information	Portage County Parks Dept. 715/346-1433 www.co.port.wi.us
County	Portage

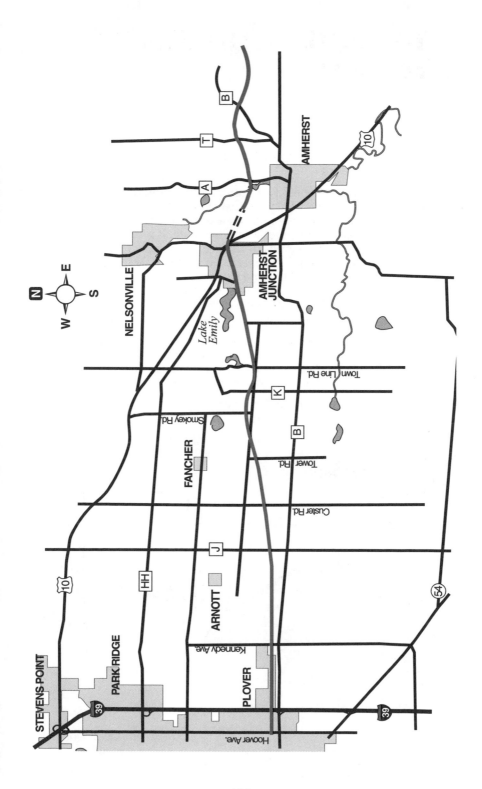

Tri-County Corridor

Length	60 miles
Surface	Ballast, cinder, crushed stone, and 9 miles of asphalt trail in Superior
Location & Setting	The Tri-County Recreation Trail is built on abandoned railbed and parallels Hwy 2 between Superior and Ashland. The trail provides a panoramic view of local farms and forests, with small communities along the route. It serves as a major connector to the hundreds of miles of recreational trail in northwest Wisconsin. It links extensive snowmobile trails throughout Douglas, Ashland, and Bayfield Counties, as well as those going as far south as the Twin Cities. The 9 mile portion of the trail in the city of Superior is known as the Osaugie Trail, and has a asphalt surface.
Getting There	The Osaugie Trail starts at 2nd Street and 2nd Avenue in Superior. The Tri-County Recreation Corridor Trail then begins at 30th Avenue. The east trailhead is located at Sanborn Avenue (Hwy 112), just north of where it intersects Hwy 137 in Ashland.
Information	Superior Parks & Recreation 715/394-0270 Tri-County Recreation Corridor Trail 800/472-6338

www.a1trails.com/rail/wi/tricounty.thml

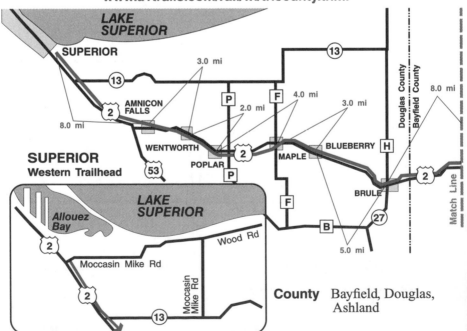

County Bayfield, Douglas, Ashland

Camping is available at Amnicon Falls State Park (36 sites) and Wanoka Lake Campground in Chequamegon National Forest.

AREA OVERVIEW

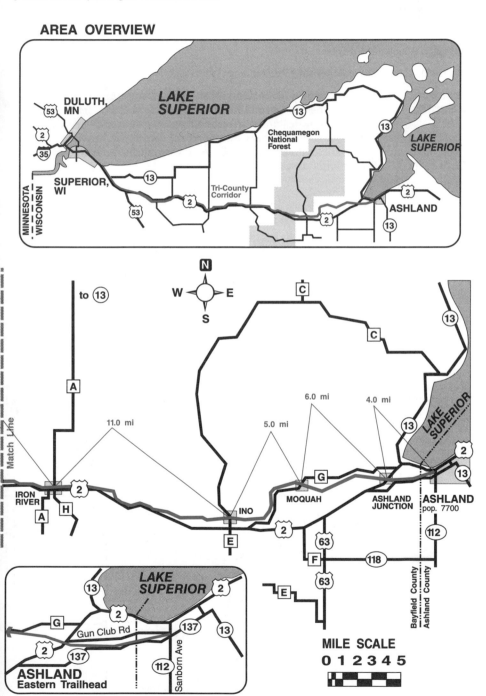

MILE SCALE
0 1 2 3 4 5

Tuscobia-Park Falls State Trail

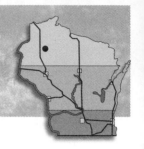

Length	74 miles
Surface	Loose gravel, cinders
Location & Setting	The trail consists of abandoned railbed and runs from Park Falls at the eastern trailhead to Turcobia, the western trailhead, and a few miles north of Rice Lake. The setting is primarily open area, woods, and small communities. Be prepared for several stream crossings. Enjoy the rugged wilderness of the Blue Hills from a nearly level terrain.
Getting There	Access the east trailhead by turning west off Hwy 13 at Division Street and proceed 5 blocks to 9th Avenue. The trail is one block south of Division Street.

Access the west trailhead by exiting Hwy 53 at Hwy 48. Proceed east to Hwy SS and then north. The trailhead begins off Hwy SS just before it passes under Hwy 53. The Country Inn restaurant is ¼ miles south. |
| **Information** | Tuscobia State Trail   715/634-6513 |
| **County** | Price, Sawyer, Washburn, Barron |

Trail parallels Hwy 48 as you pass through town. Parking, restaurant, and lodging near the trail.

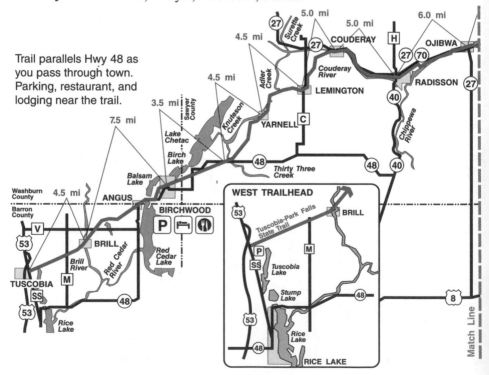

TUSCOBIA-PARK FALLS STATE TRAIL ROUTE SLIP:

Park Falls	SEGMENT	TOTAL
Kaiser Rd.	3.5	3.5
Log Creek	9.0	12.5
Draper	6.0	18.5
Loretta	1.0	19.5
Winter (HWY W)	9.0	28.5
Ojibwa	5.0	33.5
Radisson	6.0	39.5
Couderay	5.0	44.5
Lemington (HWY C)	5.0	49.5
Yarnell Rd. (N/S)	4.5	54.0
HWY 48 (E/W)	4.5	58.5
Birchwood	3.5	62.0
Brill (27th Ave.)	7.5	69.5
HWY 53	4.5	74.0

PARK FALLS EAST TRAILHEAD

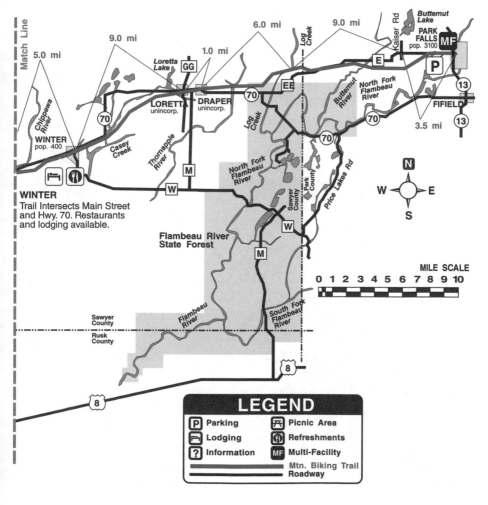

WINTER
Trail Intersects Main Street and Hwy. 70. Restaurants and lodging available.

Flambeau River State Forest

LEGEND

P	Parking	🏕	Picnic Area
🛏	Lodging	🍴	Refreshments
?	Information	MF	Multi-Facility
			Mtn. Biking Trail
			Roadway

Waukesha County Trails

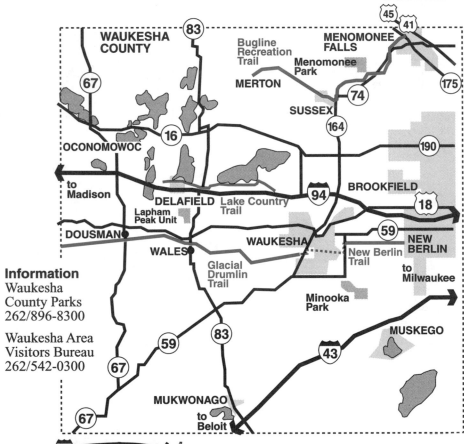

Information
Waukesha
County Parks
262/896-8300

Waukesha Area
Visitors Bureau
262/542-0300

WAUKESHA COUNTY 83

Bugline Recreation Trail

67

MERTON

MENOMONEE FALLS

Menomonee Park

45 41

175

74

16

OCONOMOWOC

SUSSEX

164

190

to Madison

DELAFIELD Lake Country Trail

Lapham Peak Unit

94

BROOKFIELD

18

DOUSMAN

WALES

WAUKESHA

59

New Berlin Trail

NEW BERLIN

Glacial Drumlin Trail

to Milwaukee

Minooka Park

MUSKEGO

59

83

43

67

MUKWONAGO

to Beloit

67

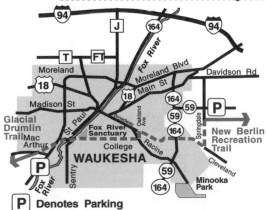

P Denotes Parking

Waukesha Bikeway Connection to the Glacial Drumlin Trail
From the New Berlin Trail, south on Springdale Road for .7 miles to Broadway. West on Broadway for 1.3 miles to Oakland Avenue, then south on Oakland Avenue for 1 block to College Avenue. Continue west on College Avenue through the Fox River Sanctuary for 1.5 miles to the glacial Drumlin trailhead. Parking and restrooms are available at the Sanctuary.

ROUTES

▬▬▬▬	Biking Trail
■ ■ ■ ■	Bikeway
▬■▬■▬	Alternate Bike Trail
••••••	Undeveloped Trail
■ ▪ ■ ▪ ■	Alternate Use Trail
= = = =	Planned Trail
▬▬▬▬	Roadway

FACILITIES

🔧	Bike Repair
△	Camping
➕	First Aid
❓	Info
🛏	Lodging
P	Parking
🏕	Picnic
⑩	Refreshments
🚺🚹	Restrooms
🏠	Shelter
🚰	Water
MF	Multi Facilities

Refreshments   First Aid
Telephone   Picnic
Restrooms   Lodging

TRAIL USES

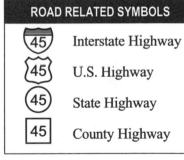

🚵	Mountain Biking
🚲	Leisure Biking
	In Line Skating
	Cross-Country Skiing
🚶	Hiking
∩	Horseback Riding
	Snowmobiling
	All Terrain Vehicles

ROAD RELATED SYMBOLS

45	Interstate Highway
45	U.S. Highway
45	State Highway
45	County Highway

AREA DESCRIPTIONS

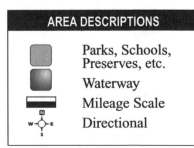

	Parks, Schools, Preserves, etc.
	Waterway
	Mileage Scale
	Directional

White River State Trail

Length	11 miles
Surface	Limestone screenings
Location & Setting	A 11 mile state trail between Elkhorn and Spring Valley Road, just west of Burlington at Springfield Valley Road by the Racine County line. It follows a former railroad bed. The trail goes past numerous bridges, scenic vistas, quaint towns, farmlands, wetlands, and through the historic village of Lyons. It also passes within 5 miles of Lake Geneva and Big Foot Beach State Park. The 2 mile stretch between Springfield and Lyons is open to horseback riding.
Getting There	The western trailhead is off Petrie Road, on the southeast edge of Elkhorn, a half mile south of the Hwy 43 and Hwy 12 junction. The eastern trailhead is off Spring Valley Road at the Racine County line.
Information	Walworth Dept. of Public Works 262/741-3114
County	www.dnr.state.wi.us

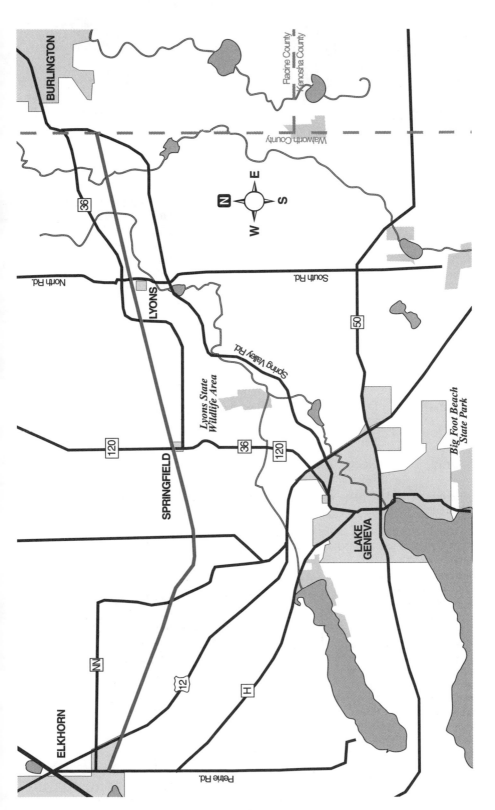

Wild Goose State Trail

Length	34.5 miles
Surface	Limestone screenings
Location & Setting	Located in southeast Wisconsin, it follows an abandoned railbed between Fond du Lac and Clyman. The trail parallels the western side of the Horicon Marsh Wildlife Area and National Wildlife Refuge. The route is tree lined with wild-flowers, woodlots, wildlife, farm fields, prairie remnants, and glacial moraines. Horseback riding is permitted on a separate horse trail in Dodge County between Hwy 60 and Minnesota Junction. Snowmobiles are permitted when conditions officially allow. Winter ATV use is permitted in Dodge County only when conditions allow.
Getting There	North trailhead: Sheboygan – at the west end of Erie Street one half mile west of Memorial Mall.
	South trailhead: Route 60, one mile east of Route 26.
Information	Dodge County Planning & Development 920/386-3700 **www.co.dodge.wi.us**
	Fond du Lac County Planning 920/929-3135
County	Dodge, Fond du Lac

Fond du Lac Bordered on the north by Lake Winnebago, the largest freshwater lake in Wisconsin. Points of interest include the 'Talking Houses and Historic Places' tour and historic Galloway House and Village.

Parking in Fond du Lac Suggestions include Marsh Haven Nature Center and the Horicon National Wildlife Refuge just east of the trail at Hwy 49, the Juneau City Park on Lincoln Street, and at the intersections of Hwy 33 and 26.

Horicon Marsh is an extinct glacial lake and the largest fresh-water cattail marsh in the United States. It's known as the "Little Everglades of the North". The marsh supports diverse wildlife and plants, including threatened species such as great egrets, bald eagles, osprey, and peregrine falcons. Horicon marsh is a major migration stopover for the Mississippi valley population of Canada geese during their travels between Hudson Bay and southern Illinois/western Kentucky. Over 100,000 descend on Horicon Marsh in the spring and fall.

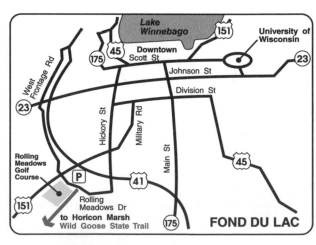

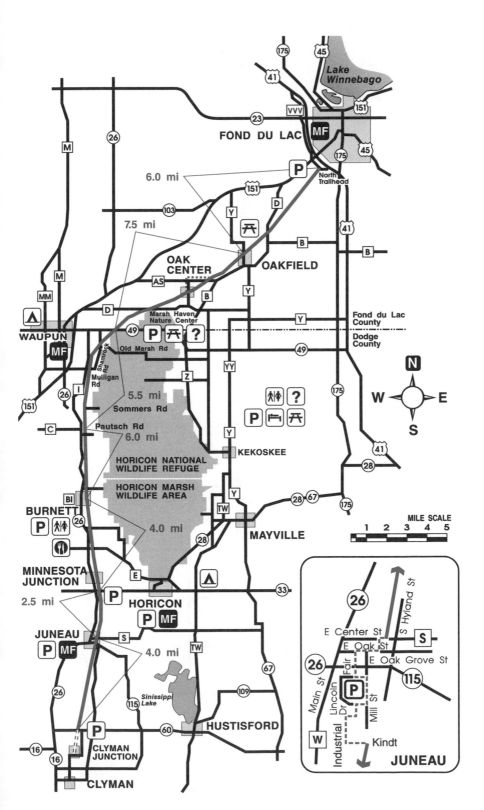

Lake Winnebago

FOND DU LAC

6.0 mi

North Trailhead

7.5 mi

OAK CENTER

OAKFIELD

Marsh Haven Nature Center

Fond du Lac County

WAUPUN

Old Marsh Rd

Dodge County

Shamrock Rd

Mulligan Rd

5.5 mi
Sommers Rd

Pautsch Rd
6.0 mi

KEKOSKEE

HORICON NATIONAL WILDLIFE REFUGE

HORICON MARSH WILDLIFE AREA

4.0 mi

MAYVILLE

BURNETT

MINNESOTA JUNCTION

2.5 mi

HORICON

JUNEAU

4.0 mi

Sinissippi Lake

HUSTISFORD

CLYMAN JUNCTION

CLYMAN

MILE SCALE
1 2 3 4 5

E Center St
S Hyland St
E Oak St
E Oak Grove St
Main St
Fair
Lincoln Dr
Mill St
Industrial
Kindt
JUNEAU

125

Wildwood Trail

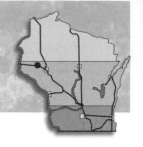

Length	7 miles
Surface	Crushed gravel, cinder, dirt
Location & Setting	The Wildwood Trail runs from the village of Woodville south to Spring Valley at the St. Croix/Pierce County line. It is being developed on railroad grade from the St. Paul, Minneapolis and Omaha Railway. The trail's length is 7 miles, with a surface varying from gravel to dirt and cinder. There have been some improvements since it was abandoned as a railbed. The setting is farm fields, pastures and woodlots.
Getting There	Woodville is just north of I-94 on Route B. The trailhead is off Cty BB.
Information	St. Croix County Parks 715/265-4613 www.co.saint-croix.wi.us
County	St. Croix

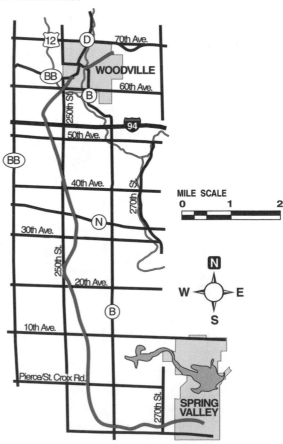

Find me a place, safe and serene,

away from the terror I see on the screen.

A place where my soul can find some peace,

away from the stress and the pressures released.

A corridor of green not far from my home

for fresh air and exercise, quiet will roam.

Summer has smells that tickle my nose

and fall has the leaves that crunch under my toes.

Beware, comes a person we pass in a while

with a wave and hello and a wide friendly smile.

Recreation trails are the place to be,

to find that safe haven of peace and serenity.

By Beverly Moore, Illinois Trails Conservancy

Wiouwash State Trail

Length	44 miles
Surface	Limestone screenings
Location & Setting	Two sections of this rail trail are complete: the 20 mile south section from the outskirts of Oshkosh to Hortonville, and the 24 mile north section from Split Rock To Birnamwood. The two sections are currently separated by a gap of 30 miles. Trail passes are required for bicyclists 18 years of age or older.

Wiouwash Trail – South Section

Length	22 miles
Location & Setting	The trail weaves through woods, marshes, farm fields, and prairies, providing trail users with a wide variety of scenery. Just off the trail in the town of Clayton is Trail Head Park, which has restrooms, picnic tables, and a large parking area.
Getting There	The south trailhead can be accessed from West Wind Road just southwest of the intersection of Hwy 41 and Hwy 110. There is Parking at the intersection of Hwy 110 and Cty Y (Sunnyview Road).

For the north trailhead, exit Hwy 45 onto Hwy M (Nash Street) for 2 blocks to Lake Shore Drive. Follow the lake for about a mile where you will find parking but no designated facilities. There is a picnic area at the Hwy 45 exit. |
| **Information** | Winnebago County Parks   920/232-1960
Outagamie County Parks   920/832-4790 |
| **County** | Winnebago, Outagamie |

Wiouwash Trail – North Section

Length	24 miles
Location & Setting	This section is located in Shawano County. The setting is rural with the trail traveling along farmland and through small communities.
Getting There	From Hortonville, continue on Hwy 45 to the village of Split Rock, or you can start your ride from Marion to Split Rock via Cty SS & S.
Information	Shawano County Parks 715/526-6766
County	Shawano

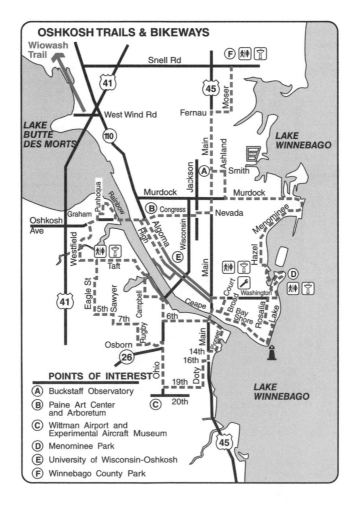

OSHKOSH TRAILS & BIKEWAYS

Wiowash Trail

Snell Rd

41

45

Moser

West Wind Rd

Fernau

110

LAKE BUTTE DES MORTS

Jackson

Main

Ashland

LAKE WINNEBAGO

A Smith

Murdock

Murdock

Punhoqua

Rainbow

Graham

B Congress

Nevada

Oshkosh Ave

Westfield

Algoma

High

Wisconsin

Menominee

Taft

E

Main

Hazel

Eagle St

Sawyer

Court

Broad

Washington

D

41

5th

7th

Campbell

Ceape

6th

Bay Shore

Rosalia

Lake

Rugby

Pioneer

Osborn

Main

14th

26

16th

Ohio

Doty

19th

POINTS OF INTEREST

A Buckstaff Observatory

20th

C

LAKE WINNEBAGO

B Paine Art Center and Arboretum

C Wittman Airport and Experimental Aircraft Museum

D Menominee Park

E University of Wisconsin-Oshkosh

45

F Winnebago County Park

Wiouwash State Trail (continued)

North Section

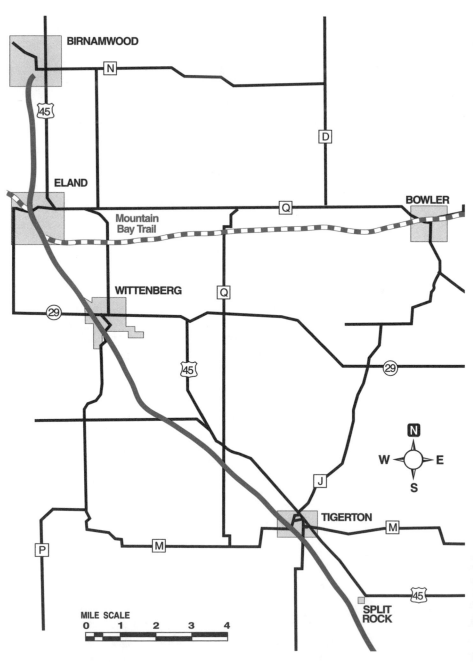

BIRNAMWOOD

N

45

D

ELAND

Mountain
Bay Trail

Q

BOWLER

WITTENBERG

Q

29

45

29

N
W   E
S

J

TIGERTON

M

M

P

SPLIT
ROCK

45

MILE SCALE
0   1   2   3   4

South Section

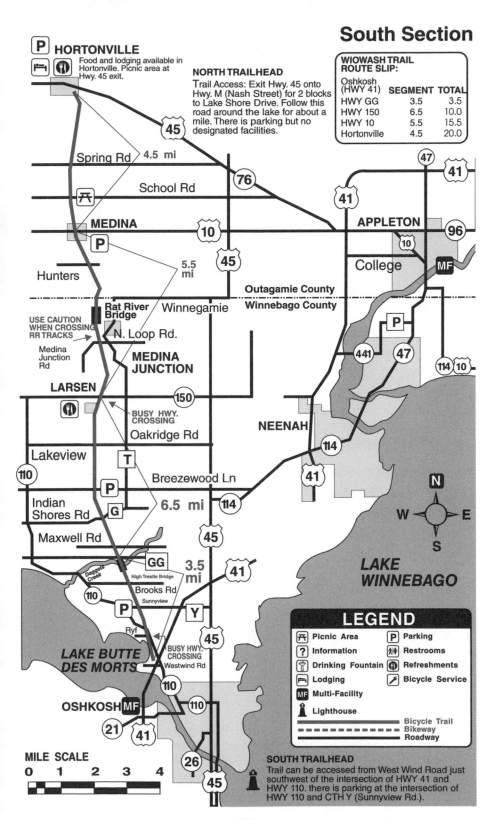

P **HORTONVILLE**
Food and lodging available in Hortonville. Picnic area at Hwy. 45 exit.

NORTH TRAILHEAD
Trail Access: Exit Hwy. 45 onto Hwy. M (Nash Street) for 2 blocks to Lake Shore Drive. Follow this road around the lake for about a mile. There is parking but no designated facilities.

WIOWASH TRAIL ROUTE SLIP:

Oshkosh (HWY 41)	SEGMENT	TOTAL
HWY GG	3.5	3.5
HWY 150	6.5	10.0
HWY 10	5.5	15.5
Hortonville	4.5	20.0

Spring Rd — 4.5 mi

School Rd

47

41

41

MEDINA — 10

APPLETON — 96

45

10

Hunters — 5.5 mi

College — MF

Outagamie County
Winnebago County

Rat River Bridge — Winnegamie

USE CAUTION WHEN CROSSING RR TRACKS

N. Loop Rd.

Medina Junction Rd

MEDINA JUNCTION

P

441 — 47

114 10

LARSEN

150

BUSY HWY. CROSSING

NEENAH

Oakridge Rd

114

Lakeview — T

110

Breezewood Ln

41

Indian Shores Rd — P — G — 6.5 mi — 114

Maxwell Rd

45

GG — 3.5 mi — 41

Daggets Creek

High Trestle Bridge

LAKE WINNEBAGO

110

Brooks Rd

Sunnyview

P — Y

Ryf

45

BUSY HWY. CROSSING

LAKE BUTTE DES MORTS

Westwind Rd

110

OSHKOSH MF

110

21 — 41

N

W — E

S

LEGEND

🪵	Picnic Area	**P**	Parking
？	Information	🚻	Restrooms
⛲	Drinking Fountain	🍴	Refreshments
🛏	Lodging	🔧	Bicycle Service
MF	Multi-Facility		
🗼	Lighthouse		

━━━ Bicycle Trail
▬ ▬ ▬ Bikeway
━━━ Roadway

MILE SCALE

0   1   2   3   4

26

45

SOUTH TRAILHEAD
Trail can be accessed from West Wind Road just southwest of the intersection of HWY 41 and HWY 110. there is parking at the intersection of HWY 110 and CTH Y (Sunnyview Rd.).

Mountain Biking Alternatives

SOUTHEAST WISCONSIN

Bong State Recreation Area

Length	12 miles
Effort Level	Easy
Setting	Level to rolling terrain. Prairie, woodlands, wetlands
Location	From Kenosha, 16 miles west on Hwy 142 to entrance. From Burlington, go 8 miles southeast on Hwy 142.
Park Office	414/878-5600

Devil's Lake State Park

Length	6.5 miles
Effort Level	Easy to difficult
Setting	A generally medium effort trail that is long, winding and grassy, with variable grades through fields, bushy areas and woods. Scenic views from the top of the East Bluff on the south end.
Park Office	608/356-8301

Harrington Beach State Park

Length	2.0 miles
Effort Level	Easy
Setting	Grassing, sand, lake shore
Location	Ten miles north of Port Washington on Hwy 43, and then east on Cty D for 1 mile.
Park Office	414/285-3015

Kettle Moraine – Northern Unit

Park Office	414/626-2116

Greenbush Recreation Area

Length	10.9 miles
Effort Level	Easy to difficult
Setting	Hills, woods, grassy areas
Location	Hwy 23 west to Kettle Moraine Drive at the small town of Greenbush, and then south for 2 miles.

New Fane Trails

Length	7.7 miles
Setting	Hills, woods, grassy areas
Location	Hwy 23 west to Kettle Moraine Drive at the small town of Greenbush, and then south for 2 miles.

Kettle Moraine – Southern Unit

Park Office   414/594-6200

John Muir Trails

Length	19.2 miles
Effort Level	Easy to difficult
Setting	Hilly, rocky, open fields, woods
Location	From Milwaukee, take Hwy 43 southwest to Hwy 20 for about 9 miles to where it joins Hwy 12. West on Hwy 12 for less than 2 miles to Cty H, and then north to the entrance. From Chicago, go northwest on Hwy 12.

Emma F. Carlin Trails

Length	9.4 miles
Effort Level	Easy to difficult
Setting	Hilly and wooded
Location	From Milwaukee, take Hwy 43 southwest to the town of Mukwonago. Pick up Cty NN north of town and proceed west for 5 miles to Eagle. Continue west on Hwy 59 for 4 miles to Carlin Trail Road, and then south to the entrance.

Lapham Peak Unit

Length	4.4 miles
Effort Level	Easy to moderate
Setting	Hills, woods, open fields
Location	From Waukesha, west on Hwy 94 for seven miles, and then south for 1 miles on Cty C.

SOUTHWEST WISCONSIN

Blue Mound State Park

Length	5.0 miles
Effort Level	Easy to difficult
Setting	Grass, Woods, steep hills
Location	One mile northwest of the town of Blue Mounds, off Hwy 18/15.
Park Office	608/437-5711

Mountain Biking Alternatives (continued)

SOUTHWEST WISCONSIN (continued)

Bluebird Springs Recreation Area

Length	8.0 miles
Effort Level	Moderate to difficult
Setting	Grassy & dirt trails with challenging, steep slopes in a private campground.
Location	From I-90, south on Hwy 16 to Cty B, then east 1.2 miles to Smith Valley Road. Continue south on Smith Valley Road south for about 3 miles to the campground.

Brown County Reforestation Camp Trails

Length	20.0 miles
Effort Level	Easy
Setting	Deep forest, gently rolling to flat.
Location	From Green Bay, north on Hwy 41/141 to Cty B, then west for 2.5 miles to Cty IR (Reforestation Road).
Park Office	Brown County Park System 920/448-4466

Governor Dodge State Park

Length	10 miles
Effort Level	Moderate
Setting	Meadows, wooded ridges and valleys
Location	Three miles north of Dodgeville on Hwy 23.
Park Office	608/935-2315

Mirror Lake State Park

Length	9.2 miles
Effort Level	Easy to moderate
Setting	Woods, gravel, sand
Location	One and a half miles southwest of Lake Delton on Ishnala Road. Exit Hwy 94 at Hwy 12 and proceed south for one mile to Fern Dell Road. There is an entrance at the Hastings Road ` intersection.
Park Office	608/254-2333

Perrot State Park
Length   6 miles
Effort Level   Moderate to difficult
Setting   Hard packed ski trails. Marshland, prairie, wooded slopes.
Location   From LaCrosse, take Hwy 35 north and then west to Hwy 93 at Centerville. Proceed south on Hwy 93 for 4.5 miles to Trempealeau. Follow the park signs. From Winona, cross the Hwy 43 bridge and take Hwy 35 east 10 miles to Centerville.
Park Office   608/534-6409

Wyalusing State Park
Length   11.6 miles
Effort Level   Easy to difficult
Setting   Woods, grassy areas, gently rolling to steep slopes.
Location   Seven miles south of Prairie Du Chien on Hwy 18, then west on Hwy C.
Park Office   608/996-2261

NORTHEAST WISCONSIN
High Cliff State Park
Length   8.2 miles
Effort Level   Easy
Setting   Woods, cliffs, lakefront
Location   Three miles south on Hwy 55 from the town of Sherwood. At High Cliff Road turn left to enter the park. Sherwood is about 12 miles southeast of Appleton.
Park Office   920/989-1106

Newport State Park
Length   12 miles
Effort level   Easy
Setting   Forest, wetlands, meadows
Location   Door County, 2 miles east of Ellison Bay on Hwy 22, and then 2 miles southeast on Cty Z.
Park Office   920/854-2500

Peninsula State Park
Length   12.8 miles
Effort Level   Easy to moderate
Setting   Forest, meadows, marsh cliffs
Location   Door County, 3 miles north of Fish Creek off Hwy 42.
Park Office   920/868-3258

Mountain Biking Alternatives (continued)

NORTHEAST WISCONSIN (continued)

Potawatomi State Park

Length	4 miles
Effort Level	Moderate
Setting	Flat to gently rolling upland terrain, bordered by steep slopes and cliffs
Location	Door County, 5 miles northwest of Sturgeon Bay. Take Hwy 42/57 west to Park Road, and then north to the park entrance.
Park Office	920/746-2890

Point Beach State Forest

Length	4 miles
Effort level	Moderate
Setting	Forest bordered by sand beaches
Location	Four miles north of Two Rivers, off Cty O.
Park Office	920/794-7480

Point Beach State Park

Length	4 miles
Effort Level	Moderate
Setting	Flat to gently rolling upland terrain, bordered by steep slopes and cliffs.
Park Office	912/794-7480

Paust's Woods Lake Resort Trails

Length	7.5 miles
Effort Level	Moderate to difficult
Setting	Forest, large granite rocks
Location	From Crivitz, west on Cty W for 12 miles to Parkway Road, then north for about 8 miles to Ranch Road. West on Ranch Road for a mile to Paust Lane, then north to the resort.
Park Office	Nicolet National Forest 715/362-1300

WEST CENTRAL

Black River State Forest

Forest Office   715/284-1440

Castle Mounds Park

Length	4.5 miles
Effort Level	Easy
Setting	Generally level with grassy surface, but a few hills.
Location	1.5 miles southeast of black River Falls on Hwy 12.

Pigeon Creek

Length	4.5 miles
Effort Level	Easy
Setting	Fairly level terrain with mostly grassy surface
Location	Twelve miles southeast of Black River Falls on Hwy 12 to Cty O, then 4 miles northeast to North Settlement Road.

Smrekar Trail

Length	7.5 miles
Effort Level	Moderate to difficult
Setting	Wooded, ridges
Location	Twelve miles southeast of Black River Falls on Hwy 12 to Cty O, then 4 miles northeast to North Settlement Road. Continue northeast.

Wildcat Trail

Length	7.5 miles
Effort Level	Moderate to difficult
Setting	Heavy woods, buttes and sandstone hills
Location	Twelve mile southeast of Black River Falls on Hwy 12 to Cty O, then 4 miles northeast to North Settlement Road. Continue northeast.

Lake Wissota State Park

Length	11 miles
Effort Level	Easy
Setting	Mostly prairie grass and plantation pines
Location	Eight miles northeast of Chippewa Falls. North on Hwy 53 to Cty 3, then east, turning right on Cty S and continue for 1.7 miles to the park entrance.
Park Office	715/382-4574

Mountain Biking
Alternatives (continued)

WEST CENTRAL (continued)

Levis/Trow Mounds Trails

Length	12.0 miles
Effort Level	Easy to difficult
Setting	Rolling terrain with many switch-backs. Scenic bluff colored outcroppings.
Location	From Merrillan, east on Hwy 95 to the trailhead just west of the Cty J junction.
Park Office	Neillsville Area Chamber 715/743-6444

Lowes Creek County Park

Length	4.9 miles
Effort Level	Easy to difficult
Setting	The West Loop is rolling and prairies. The East Loop is wooded. The trail loop between the two is flat and mostly open.
Park Office	715/839-4738

NORTH CENTRAL WISCONSIN

Langley Lake Trails

Length	15.5 miles
Effort Level	Easy
Setting	Forest, lake views, grassy surface
Location	From Hwy 45/32, west on Cty K for 7 miles to Langley Lake road and the trailhead.
Park Office	Eagle River Chamber 715/479-6400

Lumberjack Trail

Length	26 miles
Effort Level	Easy to moderate
Setting	Gently rolling, heavily wooded
Location	From Boulder Junction, south 1 mile on old Hwy K to Concora Road, or from Boulder Junction about 6 miles southeast on Cty K to the east side of White Sand Lake.

Madeline Lake Trail

Length	9.5 miles
Effort Level	Easy to moderate
Setting	Level to rolling terrain
Location	Two miles southeast of Woodruff. Take Hwy 51 to Cty J, east on Cty J to Rudolph Road and then north to the trail.
Park Office	715/356-5211

McNaughton Lake Trail

Length	7.0 miles
Effort Level	Easy
Setting	Gentle terrain with a few steep hills. Dirt and mowed grass
Location	Thirteen miles south of Woodruff. Take Hwy 47 east, through Lake Tomahawk. Turn right on Kildare Road.
Park Office	715/356-5211

Nicolet North Trails

Length	10.5 miles
Effort Level	Moderate
Setting	Forest with bog and lake views, and rolling terrain
Location	From Eagle River take Hwy 70 east for 8.5 miles to Military Road, then south on FR2181 (Butternut Lake road). East on FR2425, then south to a parking area on the west side of the road.

Nine Mile County Forest Trail

Length	18.5 miles
Effort Level	Easy to difficult
Setting	Wooded uplands, marshes, water impoundments
Location	From Wausau at Hwy 51, take Cty N west approximately 3.5 miles to Red Bud Road, and then south 1.5 miles.
Forest Office	715/847-5267

Shannon Lake Trail

Length	7.6 miles
Effort Level	Easy to moderate
Setting	Gently rolling and wooded
Location	Two and a half miles northeast of St. Germain. Take Hwy 155 to Found Lake Road. Another access is approximately 10 miles from Eagle River on Cty G.
Park Office	715/356-5211

Mountain Biking Alternatives (continued)

NORTHWEST WISCONSIN

Blue Hills Trails

Length	20.0 miles
Effort Level	Easy to difficult
Setting	East side is largely forested and hilly. The west side is more open with gentler terrain and scenic vistas.
Location	From Rice Lake, east on Cty C (becomes Cty O) about 20 miles to Fire Lane Road, then northwest past the Blue Hills Trails parking area for another 2 miles to Perch Lake Road. West to the Audie Flowage Recreation Area.
Park Office	Rush County 715/732-2113

Brule River State Forest

Length	6.0 miles
Effort Level	Easy to moderate
Setting	Rolling hills, deep forests
Location	Two miles northwest of Brule on Hwy 2, then west to the trailhead
Forest Office	715/372-4866

Cooper Falls State Park

Length	8.3 miles
Effort Level	Easy to difficult
Setting	Rolling terrain, hilly
Location	Two miles north to Mellon on Hwy 169, then 2 miles on Cty J. The trailhead is west of the main park entrance road, about .3 miles from the park office. Take the right trail split.
Park Office	715/274-5123

Flambeau River State Forest

Length	Over 100 miles
Effort Level	Easy to difficult
Setting	Forests
Location	Approximately 10 miles southwest of Park Falls, between Hwy 70 to the north and Hwy 8 to the south.
Forest Office	715/332-5271

Pines & Mines Trails

Length	23.0 miles
Effort Level	Easy to difficult
Setting	Deep forest, old mining towns and mine sites
Location	Town of Montreal on Hwy 77
Park Office	Iron County 715/561-2922

Rock Lake Trail

Length	25 miles (loops)
Effort Level	Easy to difficult
Setting	Rolling terrain, hills, forests, ridges
Location	Seven and a half miles east of Cable and 12 miles west of Clam Lake on Cty M.
Forest Office	715/634-4821

Wintergreen Trail

Length	15.4 miles
Effort Level	Moderate to difficult
Setting	Forests, upland ridges to lowland marshes
Location	Five miles east of Fifield and north of Hwy 70. Fifield is 4 miles south of Park Falls at Hwy 70 and 15.
Forest Office	715/762-2461

Cambra Trails

Chequamegon Area Mountain Bike Association (CAMBRA) 800/533-7454

Delta Cluster

Length	105 miles – loops
Effort Level	Easy to difficult; single track sections
Location	Between Iron River and Drummond

Drummond Cluster

Length	79 miles – loops
Effort Level	Easy to moderate – road sections and ski trails
Location	Drummond

Cable Cluster

Length	60 miles – loops
Effort Level	Easy to difficult
Location	South from Cable on Randysek Road for less than a mile, then east on McNaught Road to the trailhead.

Mountain Biking
Alternatives (continued)

NORTHWEST WISCONSIN (continued)

Seeley Cluster

Length	68 miles – loops
Effort Level	Moderate to difficult
Location	Seeley

Hayward Cluster

Length	34 miles – loops
Effort Level	Easy to moderate
Location	Hayward

Namakagon Cluster

Length	42 miles – loops
Effort Level	Easy to difficult
Location	Trailheads are east of Namakagon, off Hwy M.

Bed and Breakfast

Albany
Sugar River State Park Trail
Albany House
405 S. Mill Street
Albany, WI 53502
866/977-7000
www.albanyhouse.com

Oak Hill Manor B&B
401 East Main Street
Albany, WI 53502
608/862-1400
www.oakhillmanor.com

Appleton
CE Trail
Franklin Street Inn
318 E. Franklin Street
Appleton, WI 54911
888/993-1711
www.franklinstreetinn.com

Quilt N Be
300 W. Prospect Ave.
Appleton, WI 54911
888/306-8880
www.quiltingbb.com

The Roost Bed & Breakfast
1900 South Lee Street
Appleton, WI 54915
866/803-7814
www.theroostbandb.com

Ashland
Tri-County Recreation Corridor
Inn At Timber Cove
1319 Sanborn Ave.
Ashland, WI 54806
715/682-9600
www/innattimbercove.com

The Residenz
723 Chapple Avenue
Ashland, WI 54806
715/682-2425
www.residenzbb.com

Browntown
Cheese Country Recreation Trail
Honeywind Farm
W8247 County P
Browntown, WI 53522
608/325-5215

Camp Douglas
Omaha Trail
Bluff View B&B
101 Castle St.
Camp Douglas, WI 54618
608/427-3631
barb@mwt.net

Sunnyfield Farm B&B
N6692 Batko Rd
Camp Douglas, WI 54618
888/839-0232
www.sunnyfield.net

Chippewa Falls
Old Abe Trail
McGilvray's Victorian B&B
312 W. Columbia Street
Chippewa Falls, WI 54729
888/324-1893
www.megilvraysbb.com

Pleasant View B&B
16649 96th Avenue
Chippewa Falls, WI 54729
866/947-7682
www.pleasantviewbb.com

Dodgeville
Military Ridge State Park Trail
The Grandview
4717 Miess Road
Dodgeville, WI 53533
608/935-3261
www.grandview.bb.com

Eau Claire
Chippewa River Trail
Apple Tree Inn
6700 Hwy 53 South
Eau Claire, WI 54701
800/347-9598
www.appletreeinnbb.com

Bed and Breakfast (continued)

The Atrium B&B
5572 Prill Road
Eau Claire, WI 54701
888/773-0094
www.atriumbb.com

Otter Creek Inn
2536 Hwy 12
Eau Claire, WI 54701
866/832-2945
www.ottercreekinn.com

Elroy
400 Trail
Sparta Trail
Omaha Trail
East View B&B
33620 County P Road
Elroy, WI 53929
608/43-7564
www.outspokinadventures.com/
eastview.ht

Fish Creek
Peninsula State Park
The Juniper Inn
N9432 Maple Grove Road
Fish Creek WI 54212
800/218-6960
www.juniperinn.com

Thorp House Inn & Cottages
4135 Bluff Lane
Fish Creek, WI 54212
920/868-2444
www.thorphouseinn.com

The Whistling Swan Inn
4192 Main Street
Fish Creek, WI 54212
888/277-4289
www.whistlingswan.com

The White Gull Inn
4225 Main Street, POB 160
Fish Creek, WI 54212
800/624-1987
www.whitegullinn.com

Fort Atkinson
Glacial River Trail
La Grange Bed & Breakfast
1050 East St.
Fort Atkinson, WI 53538
920/563-1421
www.1928barn.com

The Lamp Post Inn
408 South Main Street
Fort Atkinson, WI 53538
920/563-6561
www.thelamppostinn.com

Green Bay
Fox River Trail
Mountain-Bay Trail
Astor House
637 S. Monroe Avenue
Green Bay, WI 54301
888/303-6370
www.astorhouse.com

Hazelhurst
Bearskin State Trail
Hazelhurst Inn
6941 Hwy 51
Hazelhurst, WI 54531
715/356-6571
hzhrstbb@networth.net

Horicon
Wild Goose State Trail
Honeyhbee Inn B&B
611 East Walnut Street
Horicon, WI 53032
920/485-4835
www.honeybeeinn.com

Hortonville
Wiouwash State Park Trail
Serenity Hills B&B
W10233 Hwy TT-Prestige Lane
Hortonville, WI 54944
920/779-9991

Janesville

Janesville's Trail

Scarlett House
835 E. Court Street
Janesville, WI 53545
608/754-8000
www.scarletthouse.com

Kendall

Elroy-Sparta State Trail

Cabin at Trails End
23009 Knollwood Road
Kendall, WI 54638
608/427-3877
www.mwt.net

La Crosse

La Crosse River Trail

The Celtic Inn
924 Cass Street
La Crosse, WI 54601
877/870-0020
adele.martin@charter.net

Four Gables Bed & Breakfast
W5648 US Hwy 14-61
La Crosse, WI 54601
608/787-1982
www.bedandbreakfast.com

Wilson Schoolhouse Inn
W5718 Hwy 14-61
La Crosse, WI 54601
608/787-1982
www.wilsonschoolhouseinn.com

Lake Mills

Glacial Drumlin State Trail

The Fargo Mansion Inn
406 Mulberry St.
Lake Mills, WI 53551
926/648-3654
www.fargomansion.com

Madison

Military Ridge State Park Trail
Glacial Drumlin State Trail
Capitol City Trail

Annie's Garden Bed & Breakfast
2117 Sheridan Drive
Madison, WI 53704
608/244-2224
www.bbinternet.com/annies

Arbor House
3402 Monroe Street
Madison, WI 53711
608/238-2981
www.bbinternet.com/annies

Canterbury Inn
315 W. Gorham at State
Madison, WI 53703
800/838-3850
www.madisoncanterbury.com

Collins House Bed and Breakfast
704 E. Gorham St.
Madison, WI 53703
608/255-4230
www.collinshouse.com

Mansion Hill Inn
424 N. Pinckney Street
Madison, WI 53709
800/798-9070
www.mansionhillinn.com

The Parsonage
PO Box 70707
Madison, WI 53708
877/517-9869
www.parsonagebandb.com

The Speckled Hen Inn
5525 Portage Road
Madison, WI 53704
877/670-4844
www.speckledhenninn.com

Medford

Pine Line Recreation Trail

Gibson House LLC
507 South Gibson Street
Medford, WI 54451
715/748-5019

Menomonie

Red Cedar State Park Trail

Cedar Trail Guesthouse
E4761 County Road C
Menomonie, WI 54751
866/6664-8828
www.cedartrailguesthouse.com

Oaklawn Bed & Breakfast
423 Technology Drive
Menomonie, WI 54751
866/235-5296
www.oaklawnbnb.com

Bed and Breakfast (continued)

Milwaukee
Oak Leaf Trail
Hank Aaron State Park Trail
The Acanthus Inn B&B
3009 W Highland blvd.
Milwaukee, WI 53208
877/468-8740
www.acanthusinn.prodigybiz.com

The Brumder Mansion B&B
3046 W. Wisconsin Avenue
Milwaukee, WI 53208
866/793-3676
www.brumdermansion.com

Minocqua
Bearskin State Trail
Sills Lakeshore B&B
130 Lakeshore Drive
Minocqua, WI 54548
715/356-3384
www.sillslakeshorebandb.com

Tamarack B&B Lodge
7950 Bo-di-Lac Drive
Minocqua, WI 54548
715/356-7124
www.tamarackbandb.com

Whitehaven B&B
1077 Hwy F
Minocqua, WI 54548
715/356-9097
www.whitehavenbandb.com

Mount Horeb
Military Ridge State Park Trail
Arbor Rose Bed & Breakfast
200 North Second Street
Mount Horeb, WI 53572
608/437-1108
www.arborrosebandb.com

Othala Valley Inn & Cabin
3192 JG-North
Mount Horeb, WI 53572
608/437-2141
www.othalavalley.com

Onalaska
Great River State Trail
LaCrosse River Trail
Lumber Baron Inn
421 2nd Avenue, N
Onalaska, WI 54560
608/781-8938
lumberbaroninwi@aol.com

Platteville
Pecatonica State Trail
Walnut Ridge
2238 Hwy A
Platteville, WI 53818
608/348-9359
www.walnutridgewi.com

Plymouth
Old Plank Road Trail
52 Stafford – An Irish Guest House
52 Stafford Street
Plymouth, WI 53073
800/421-4667
www.classicinnsofwisconsin.com

B.L. Nutt Inn
632 East Main Street
Plymouth, WI 53073
920/892-8566
www.blinternet.com/blnut

Hillwind Farm B&B Inn
N 4922 Hillwind Road
Plymouth, WI 53073
877/892-2199
www.hillwindfarm.com

Spring Tuilip Cottage
N4502 County Road S
Plymouth, WI 53073
920/892-2101
www.springtulip.com

Reedsburg
400 Trail
Lavina Inn
325 3rd Street
Reedsburg, WI 53959
608/524-6706
www.lavinainn.com

Parkview Bed & Breakfast
211 North Park Street
Reedsburg, WI 53959
608/524-4333
www.parkviewbb.com

Pine Grove Park B&B
52720 Hwy V
Reedsburg, WI 53959
866/524-0071
www.pinegroveparkbb.com

Rice Lake
Tuscobia-Park Falls State Trail
Spring Creek Bed & Breakfast
1974 23rd St.
Rice Lake, WI 54868
877/215-1257
www.springcreekbandb.com

Richland Center
Pine River Trail
Lamb's Inn B&B
23761 Misslich Road
Richland Center, WI 53581
608/585-4301
www.lambs-inn.com

Shawano
Mountain-Bay Trail
Five Keys Bed & Breakfast
103 S. Franklin St.
Shawano, WI 54166
715/526-5567
fivekeys@frontier.net

Sheboygan
Old Plank Road Trail
Brownstone Inn
1227 N 7th Street
Sheboygan, WI 53081
877/279-6786
www.brownstoneinn.com

English Manor B&B
632 Michigan Avenue
Sheboygan, WI 53081
800/557-5277
www.english-manor.com

Gramma Lori's B&B
W1681 Garton Road
Sheboygan, WI 53083
800/595-1029
www.grammalori.com

Siren
Gandy Dancer Trail
Lilac Village Bed & Breakfast
7665 Bradley Street
Siren, WI 54872
888/891-1207
www.lilacb-b.com

Sparta
Elroy-Sparta State Trail
Lacrosse River Trail
Cranberry Country Bed & Breakfast
114 W. Montgomery Street
Sparta, WI 54656
888/208-4354
www.cranberrycountrybedand
breakfast.com

Franklin Victorian Bed & Breakfast
220 E. Franklin Street
Sparta, WI 54656
888/59403822
www.franklinvictorianbb.com

Grapevine Log Cabins
19149 Jade Road
Sparta, WI 54656
608/269-3619
www.grapevinelogcabins.com

Justin trails B&B Resort
7452 Kathryn Ave. on Cty J
Sparta, WI 54656
800/488-4521
www.justintrails.com

Strawberry Lace Inn
603 N. Water Street
Sparta, WI 54656
608/269-7878
www.spartan.org/sbl

Spring Green
Pine River Trail
Hill Street B&B
353 West Hill Street
Spring Green, WI 53588
608/588-7751
www.hillstreetbb.com

Sturgeon Bay
Ahnapee State Trail
Peninsula State Park
The black Walnut Guest House
454 North Seventh Avenue
Sturgeon Bay, WI 54235
920/743-8892
www.blackwalnut-gh.com

Bed and Breakfast (continued)

Colonial Gardens Bed & Breakfast
344 N 3rd Ave.
Sturgeon Bay, WI 54235
920/746-9192
www.colgardensbb.com

Garden Gate B&B
434 North Third Ave.
Sturgeon Bay, WI 54235
877/743-9618
www.gardengateb-b.com

The Gray Goose B&B
4258 Bay Shore Drive
Sturgeon Bay, WI 54235
877/280-4258
www.ggoosebb.com

Inn at Cedar Crossing
336 Louisiana Street
Sturgeon Bay, WI 54235
920/743-4200
www.innatcedarcrossing.com

Inn the Pines B&B
4750 Bay Shore Drive
Sturgeon Bay, WI 54239
920/743-8319
www.innthepinesbb.com

The Little Harbor Inn
5100 Bay Shore Drive
Sturgeon Bay, WI 54235
877/462-6559
www.littleharborinn.com

Quiet Cottage B&B
4608 GliddenDrive
Sturgeon Bay, WI 54235
920/743-4526
www.quietcottage.com

Reynolds House B&B
111 S. 7th Avenue
Sturgeon Bay, WI 54235
877/269-7401
www.reynoldshousebandb.com

The Sawyer House B&B
101 S. Lansing Avenue
Sturgeon, WI 54235
888/746-1614
www.bbonline.com/wi/sawyer

Scofield House
908 Michigan St.
Sturgeon Bay, WI 54235
888/463-0204
www.scofieldhouse.com

White Lace Inn
16 N 5th Ave.
Sturgeon Bay, WI 54235
877/948-5223
www.whitelaceinn.com

Whitefish Bay Farm Bed & Breakfast
3831 Clark Lake Road
Sturgeon Bay, WI 54235
920/743-1560
www.whitefishbayfarm.com

Tomahawk
Hiawatha Bike Trail
Eagles Rest Bed & Breakfast
N9899 Anglers Avenue
Tomahawk, WI 54487
715/453-7515
www.eaglerest-bb.com

Wausau
Mountain-Bay Trail
Everest Inn
601 McIndoe Street
Wausau, WI 54403
715/848-5651
www.everestinn.com

Rosenberry Inn
511 Franklin Street
Wausau, WI 54403
800/336-3799
www.rosenberryinn.com

Stewart Inn
521 Grant Street
Wausau, WI 54403
715/849-5858
www.stewartinn.com

Wilton
Elroy-Sparta State Trail
Rice's Whispering Pines
22131 Cty Hwy M
Wilton, WI 54670
608/435-6531

County to Trail Index

County to Trail (continued)

Oconto .... Oconto County Recreation Trail
Oneida .... Bearskin State Trail
Oshkosh .... Wiouwash State Park Trail
Outagaimie .... CE Trail
Ozaukee........................... Ozaukee Interurban Trail
Polk .... Gandy Dancer Trail
Portage .... Green Circle Trail
Portage .... Tomorrow River State Trail
Price................................. Tuscobia-Park Falls State Trail
Price................................. Pine Line Recreation Trail
Racine.............................. M.R.K. Trail
Racine.............................. Racine County Trails
Racine.............................. North Shore Trail - Racine County
Richland .... Pine River Trail
Rock................................. Janesville's Trails
Sauk................................. 400 Trail
Sauk................................. Pine River Trail
Sawyer .... Tuscobia-Park Falls State Trail
Shawano.......................... Mountain-Bay Traill
Shawano.......................... Wiouwash State Park Trail
Sheboygan .... Old Plank Road Trail
St. Croix.......................... Wildwood Trail
Taylor .... Pine Line Recreation Trail
Trempealeau.................... Great River State Trail
Trempealeau.................... Buffalo River State Recreation Trail
Vernon .... Hillsboro State Park Trail
Vilas .... BATS - Crystal Lakes Trail
Walworth.......................... White River State Trail
Washburn .... Tuscobia-Park Falls State Trail
Waukesha .... New Berlin Recreational Trail
Waukesha .... Waukesha County Trails
Waukesha .... Bugline Recreation Trail
Waukesha .... Glacial Drumlin State Trail
Waukesha .... Lake Country Recreation Trail
Waupaca.......................... Wiouwash State Park Trail
Winnebago .... Mascoutin Valley State Trail
Winnebago .... Wiouwash State Park Trail

City to Trail Index

City to Trail (continued)

152

153

Sturgeon Bay	Peninsula State Park
Sturgeon Bay	Potawatomi State Park
Sugar Bush	Wiouwash State Park Trail
Sullivan	Glacial Drumlin State Trail
Summit Lake	Parrish Highlands
Superior	After Hours Ski Trail - Brule River SF
Superior	Oliver-Wrenshall Trail
Superior	Osaugie Trail
Superior	Saunders State Trail
Superior	Tri-County Recreation Corridor Trail
Suring	Dusty Trails
Suring	Oconto County Recreation Trail
Sussex	Bugline Recreation Trail
Thiensville	Ozaukee Interurban Trail
Thunder Mountain	Paust's Woods Lake Resort Trail
Tigerton	Embarrass River Park
Tigerton	Tigerton Trails
Tigerton	Wiouwash State Park Trail
Tomahawk	Harrison Hills
Tomahawk	Hiawatha Trail
Tomahawk	Underdown Trail
Townsend	Jones Springs Area Trail
Townsend	Oconto County Recreation Trail
Trempealeau	Great River State Trail
Tuscobia	Tuscobia-Park Falls State Trail
Two Rivers	Point Beach State Forest
Union Center	400 Trail
Union Center	Hillsboro State Park Trail
Verona	Badger State Trail
Verona	Capitol City State Trail
Verona	Military Ridge State Park Trail
Wabeno	Ed's Lake National Recreation Area
Wales	Glacial Drumlin State Trail
Washburn	Teuton Trail
Washburn	Valkyrie North Trail
Waterford	Burlington Trail
Waterford	Racine County Trails
Waterford	Waterford/Wind Lake Trail
Waukesha	Glacial Drumlin State Trail
Waukesha	New Berlin Recreational Trail
Waukesha	Waukesha County Trails
Waupaca	Hartman Creek State Park
Waupun	Wild Goose State Trail
Wausau	Council Grounds State Park
Wausau	Mountain-Bay Traill
Wausau	Nine Mile County Forest Trails
Wauwatosa	Menomonee River Trail - Milw Cnty
Webster	Gandy Dancer Trail
Wentworth	Tri-County Recreation Corridor Trail
West Allis	Menomonee River Trail - Milw Cnty
West Allis	Root River Bicycle Trail - Milw Cnty
West Salem	LaCrosse River Trail
Westboro	Pine Line Recreation Trail
Weston	Mountain-Bay Traill
Whiting	Green Circle Trail
Whittlesey	Pine Line Recreation Trail
Wilton	Elroy-Sparta State Trail
Winona, MN	Perrot State Park
Winter	Flambeau River State Forest
Winter	Oxbo Trails - Flambeau River St Forest
Winter	Tuscobia-Park Falls State Trail
Wisconsin Dells	Devils Lake State Park
Wisconsin Dells	Mirror Lake State Park
Wittenberg	Wiouwash State Park Trail
Wonewoc	400 Trail
Woodruff	Lumberjack Trail (BATS)
Woodruff	Madeline Lake Trail
Woodruff	McNaughton Lake Trails
Woodruff	Raven Trails
Woodville	Wildwood Trail
Wyalusing	Wyalusing State Park
Yarnell	Tuscobia-Park Falls State Trail

Index

Index (continued)

American Bike Trails publishes and distributes maps, books and guides for the bicyclist. For others book and map selections visit our website

American Bike Trails

w w w . a b t r a i l s . c o m